Doubts
and Loves

Richard Holloway was Bishop of Edinburgh and Primus of the Scottish Episcopal Church. A former Gresham Professor of Divinity and Chairman of the Joint Board of the Scottish Arts Council and Scottish Screen, he is a fellow of the Royal Society of Edinburgh. *Leaving Alexandria* won the PEN/Ackerley Prize and was shortlisted for the Orwell Prize. Holloway has written for many newspapers in Britain, including the *Times*, *Guardian*, *Observer*, *Herald* and *Scotsman*. He has also presented many series for the BBC television and radio; his latest book, *Waiting for the Last Bus*, originated as a five-part series on Radio 4 in 2016.

T0266373

Also by Richard Holloway

Let God Arise (1972)
New Vision of Glory (1974)
A New Heaven (1979)
Beyond Belief (1981)
Signs of Glory (1982)
The Killing (1984)
The Anglican Tradition (ed.) (1984)
Paradoxes of Christian Faith and Life (1984)
The Sidelong Glance (1985)
The Way of the Cross (1986)
Seven to Flee, Seven to Follow (1986)
Crossfire: Faith and Doubt in an Age of Certainty (1988)
The Divine Risk (ed.) (1990)
Another Country, Another King (1991)
Who Needs Feminism? (ed.) (1991)
Anger, Sex, Doubt and Death (1992)
The Stranger in the Wings (1994)
Churches and How to Survive Them (1994)
Behold Your King (1995)
Limping Towards the Sunrise (1996)
Dancing on the Edge (1997)
Godless Morality: Keeping Religion Out of Ethics (2001)
On Forgiveness: How Can We Forgive the Unforgiveable? (2002)
Looking in the Distance: The Human Search for Meaning (2004)
How to Read the Bible (2006)
Between the Monster and the Saint: Reflections on the Human Condition (2008)
Leaving Alexandria: A Memoir of Faith and Doubt (2012)
A Little History of Religion (2016)
Waiting for the Last Bus: Reflections on Life and Death (2017)

Doubts and Loves

What is Left of Christianity

RICHARD HOLLOWAY

CANONGATE

This Canons edition published in Great Britain, the USA and Canada in 2019 by
Canongate Books

Distributed in the USA by Publishers Group West and in Canada by
Publishers Group Canada

First published in Great Britain in 2001 by Canongate Books Ltd, 14 High
Street, Edinburgh EH1 1TE

canongate.co.uk

1

British Library Cataloguing-in-Publication Data
A catalogue record for this book is available on
request from the British Library

ISBN 978 1 78689 392 5

Typeset by Palimpsest Book Production Ltd, Falkirk, Stirlingshire

Printed and bound in Great Britain by Clays Ltd, Elcograf S.p.A.

For Annie

with love

From the place where we are right
flowers will never grow
in the Spring.

The place where we are right
is hard and trampled
like a yard.

But doubts and loves
dig up the world
like a mole, a plough.
And a whisper will be heard in the place
where the ruined
house once stood.

Yehuda Amichai

Contents

PART THREE

What is Left of Christianity

Preface

Two events prompted me to write this book. The more immediate was a letter from the philosopher Mary Warnock to Jamie Byng of Canongate. Jamie had sent Lady Warnock a copy of my book *Godless Morality*, hoping that she might offer it a word of commendation. In her reply she praised my book warmly, but she ended her letter with these words: 'I personally was sorry that *Godless Morality* ended where it did. I had hoped that in the epilogue there would be a discussion, however brief, of the role of religion, once it is detached from being the foundation of the moral.' This book responds to that invitation with the paradoxical suggestion that it is the moral passion that is the enduringly valuable part of the Christian religion.

But I now recognise that there was another element at work in me while I was writing it, and that was the memory of the Lambeth Conference of 1998. Every ten years, Anglican bishops from throughout the world meet at Canterbury to plot a course for the Anglican Communion for the following decade. In the event, Lambeth 1998 turned out to be the most traumatic experience of my life. The hot topic was the status of homosexuals in the Church. I went to Canterbury naïvely expecting that we would craft a classic Anglican compromise that would allow us to go on working together till some kind of creative consensus emerged in the future. In the event, the debate on the subject turned into an ugly rout, with the vast majority of bishops passing a resolution that condemned homosexuals as sinful. But it was the tone of the debate that was devastating. It was filled with a hateful glee that prompted one English bishop to liken it to a Nuremberg rally. To me it was like stumbling on a lynching organised by your own brothers. Looking back, I can now see that something profound happened to me during those hours that has radically altered my attitude to Christianity.

The shift started one lunch time during the conference, which was held on the campus of the University of Kent. Anticipating the debate, a group of Christians mounted a demonstration, holding up banners of the sort that gay and lesbian people are familiar with: *No sodomite can enter the kingdom of heaven, Abandon your evil practices or God will smite you.* My wife got hold of their leaflets and threw them in the nearest bin; but the thing that both heartened and saddened me was the action of a group of students who politely told the demonstrators how offensive and out of place their attitudes were in a university that prized human rights and personal freedom. They were answered with texts from the Bible. Puzzled, the students tried again to explain to the demonstrators how abusive and insulting their presence was. Again they were answered from the Bible. Finally, the students shrugged their shoulders and wandered off. I don't know what these students' beliefs were, but I am fairly certain that their encounter with Christianity that day scandalised them. They had met blind prejudice and ugly hatred paraded in the name of Jesus, and they had rejected them.

This growing sense in me that certain aspects of Christianity were becoming a scandal to the young was reinforced the day after the debate. A few of us at the conference, not many, had worn a rainbow ribbon to signify our commitment to the cause. After the debate, the ribbons suddenly sprouted – on the breasts of the young people who served food to us in the dining hall. They wore the ribbons as quiet badges of protest against a religious culture that had trampled on one of their most fundamental ethical values, which is not simply tolerance for, but celebration of, the wonderful variety of humanity. Again I sensed a gulf of understanding and moral sensibility between the conference and the young people who graced it with their work on our behalf. This time, it was courageous, though politely silent, witness against injustice.

It is tragic that the religion that grew round the remembrance of Jesus of Nazareth should have become the vehicle of such hatred and intolerance. This book tries to show how that happened and why it is such a perversion of the angry pity of Jesus. It has been written in order to reclaim that pity in the task of constructing a new understanding of Christianity for our time.

Acknowledgements

I would like to thank Jamie Byng of Canongate for his enthusiastic support and Mairi Sutherland for her help in editing the book.

The publishers have generously given permission to use quotations from the following copyrighted works. From 'From the Place Where We Are Right' in *Selected Poetry* by Yehuda Amichai. Reprinted by permission of Faber and Faber. From 'The Circus Animals' Desertion' and 'The Second Coming' in *The Poems* by W.B. Yeats. Reprinted by permission of A.P. Watt Ltd on behalf of Michael B. Yeats, in the UK. Reprinted with the permission of Scribner, a Division of Simon & Schuster, Inc., from *The Collected Works of W.B. Yeats, Volume 1: The Poems, Revised*, edited by Richard J. Finneran. Copyright ©1940 by Georgie Yeats, copyright renewed ©1968 by Bertha Georgie Yeats, Michael Butler Yeats and Anne Yeats, in the US. From 'Into My Heart an Air that Kills' in *Poetry and Prose: A Selection* by A.E. Housman, published by Hutchinson (1972), copyright ©in this edition F.C. Horwood, 1971. Reprinted by permission of The Society of Authors as Literary Representatives of the Estate of A.E. Housman. From 'Luke XXIII' translated by Mark Strand from *Selected Poems* by Jorge Luis Borges, edited by Alexander Coleman, copyright ©1999 by Maria Kodoma. Used by permission of Viking Penguin, a division of Penguin Putnam Inc., and Penguin Books Ltd. 'This Loafer' by C. Day Lewis: *The Complete Poems* by C. Day Lewis, published by Sinclair-Stevenson (1992), copyright ©1992 in this edition, and the Estate of C. Day Lewis. Used by permission of The Random House Group Limited. 'So Many Summers' from *The Collected Poems* by Norman MacCaig published by Chatto and Windus. Used by permission of The Random House Group Limited. From 'Draft of a Reparation Agreement' by Dan Pagis in *Modern Poems on the Bible* edited by David Curzon, copyright ©1994 by David Curzon. Reproduced by permission of The Jewish Publication Society. Excerpt from pages 45, 49–51 and 112 of *The Dynamics of Faith* by Paul Tillich published by HarperCollins (1958), copyright © 1957 by Paul Tillich, renewed ©1985 by Hannah Tillich. Reprinted by permission of HarperCollins Publishers, Inc. Excerpts from pages 200 and 201 of *The Essential Tillich* by Paul Tillich, published by The University of Chicago Press (1987), copyright ©1987 by F. Forrester Church. Reprinted by permission of The University of Chicago Press. Excerpts from *The Last of the Just* by André Schwarz-Bart, published by Penguin UK (1977), copyright ©Editions du Seuil 1959, English translation copyright ©Atheneum House Inc., 1960. Used by permission of Editions du Seuil. Excerpts from pages 105, 292 and 424 of *The Historical Jesus: The Life of a Mediterranean Jewish Peasant* by John Dominic Crossan, published by HarperCollins (1992), copyright ©1992 by John Dominic Crossan. Reprinted by permission of HarperCollins Publishers, Inc. Excerpts from *Essays in Understanding 1930–1954*, copyright ©1994 by The Literary Trustees of Hannah Arendt Bluecher, Jerome Kohn, Trustee, reprinted by permission of Harcourt, Inc. Excerpts from *The Quest of the Historical Jesus* by Albert Schweitzer, published by SCM Press (First Complete Edition, 2000). Reprinted by permission of SCM Press. Excerpt from *Errata* by George Steiner, published by Phoenix (1997), copyright © 1997 by George Steiner. Reprinted by permission of Weidenfeld and Nicolson.

PART ONE

The Shaking of the Foundations

All changed, changed utterly
W.B. Yeats, 'Easter 1916'

CHAPTER ONE

The End of Christianity

Some years ago I copied into my note book an aphorism from a Russian writer called V.V. Rozanov: 'All religions will pass, but this will remain: simply sitting in a chair and looking in the distance.' I would like to reverse Rozanov's claim and suggest that religion will remain as long as we sit in that chair looking in the distance. Another way of expressing the same thought is to use the vocabulary of the German theologian Paul Tillich, who did his greatest work in the United States after the Second World War. Tillich said that, in addition to the ordinary matters that preoccupy us, our humanity asks deep questions about the meaning of life. He called this our 'ultimate concern' and the way we respond to it is what we call religion, even though that word has become exclusively associated in people's minds with the supernatural answer to the question. Even if we reply that life has no final meaning, we are still offering that as an answer to our ultimate concern. In fact, this is the reply that is given by the scientist Richard Dawkins: 'Nature is not cruel, only pitilessly indifferent. This is one of the hardest lessons for humans to learn. We cannot admit that things might be neither good nor evil, neither cruel nor kind, but simply callous – indifferent to all suffering, lacking all purpose.'[1] This echoes something that Nietzsche wrote: 'Becoming aims at nothing and achieves nothing.'[2] These replies to the question repudiate the idea that there is any kind of supernatural meaning out there beyond us, but the idea of the ultimate meaninglessness of the universe is itself a response to our concern. Whether it is paradox or irony, the discovery of non-meaning or nihilism is itself a kind of meaning, if only because it means something to *us*, is something we ourselves read from the reality that confronts us. Just as interesting as the answers that Nietzsche and Dawkins give is the fact that they themselves are so passionately engaged in wrestling with the question. It is in the nature of humans to do this; in us, life has started to ask questions about itself. The religious quest is the deepest passion of our nature, because it is prompted by our ultimate concern. Unfortunately, like many aspects of our history, religion has been dominated by special interest groups who claimed that only their answers were true and that everyone else was in error. It is not surprising that this has happened: it is just another example of how the world ran itself for so long. Those in authority not only organised things to suit themselves, they interpreted things to suit themselves. It didn't matter what the system was, as long as they called the shots.

The folly of subjecting the religious passion to the politics of power is that it cannot be controlled in this way and refuses to be subject to external direction. I suspect that this is what the writer and film-maker Dennis Potter meant when he said just before his death: 'Religion to me has always been the wound not the bandage.'[3] This is a particularly difficult statement for religious officials to live with, especially if they work for religions of salvation. By definition, religions of salvation are in the bandage business; they have come to heal our wounds. They do not sit alongside us in the chair looking in the distance, comparing points of view; they want to protect us from what we might discover for ourselves, by telling us what the official view is and how dangerous it will be for us if we do not accept it. Or, to mix the metaphor slightly, they want to sell us their special spectacles, which have been theologically tested by experts to give us maximum power for long-distance looking. Given the extraordinary energy and variety of the human species, none of this should surprise us, but buyers should always beware of sellers. By definition, sellers want to move their product, whether it is a Mercedes or a metaphysic. To punish the metaphor a little longer, in the culture of global capitalism everything has become a commodity, including religion. The most blatant exponents of religious consumerism are North American television evangelists, the best of whom are brilliant salespersons. But even the subtler and more traditional religions try to push their brands. None of this would particularly matter if it were a case of the rival systems inviting us to view reality from where they were sitting: 'Come, try our view and see if you'd like to build your dwelling place at our bend in the river.' Though something like that is beginning to happen today, in the past, religion, like everything else, was dealt with in an authoritarian way. We were told, for our own good, what to think and what to look at; and we were told, for our own good, what not to think and what not to look at. And because religious leaders believed they were dealing with momentous issues that determined eternal destinations, religions tended to be at war with each other. It is no accident that the vocabulary of religious vituperation is so gross, particularly in the Christian tradition and even more particularly in the long feud between Catholics and Protestants. We get riled with each other when it is difficult if not impossible to establish the truth in disputed areas. We don't beat each other up over multiplication tables, but we get very agitated about religion and politics, because it is impossible to establish their incontrovertible truth.

The fascinating thing about our own day is that our attitude to these matters is beginning to change. If I can use the Rozanov metaphor one last time: today we positively revel in and celebrate the fact that there are almost as many chairs for distance-gazing as there are people to sit in them. Today there is no universally accepted answer to the question posed by our ultimate concern. The dominant characteristic of what is called post-modernity is the absence of agreement on the core meanings and values that undergird the human experience. Scholars call these underground streams of value and meaning 'metanarratives' and they tell us that the main characteristic of our society is its lack of agreement on how to understand and order human communities. In their language, we have no common metanarrative. We describe our society today as 'multicultural' and its values as 'plural'. The leaders of most religious institutions deplore this situation, for fairly obvious reasons. They talk contemptuously of 'pick and mix' Christians or 'cafeteria Catholics' who take what they want from traditional religious systems and ignore what is not congenial. While unattractive, their dyspepsia is understandable. After all, if you are invested in the proclamation of a particular system of meaning and value, which you believe to be not one among many, but the only true and saving one, then you are bound to be disturbed by the new plural culture. Religious officials feel the way all monopolists feel when competition invades their market place: they resent it, precisely because it threatens their dominance. Another important characteristic of post-modernity, which is reflected in effective business ventures, is the flattening of hierarchies and the sharing of patterns of governance. Though still more honoured in theory than in practice, there is also a commitment to equal treatment for women and sexual and ethnic minorities. All of this is in marked contrast to life in traditional religious systems, such as Christianity.

Like an ancient galleon that has spent ages at sea, Christianity is encrusted with customs and attitudes acquired on its voyage through the centuries and it is making the tragic mistake of confusing the accidents of theological and cultural history with eternal truth. Callum G. Brown in his book, *The Death of Christian Britain,* claims that the single most important element in the free-fall in church attendance in Britain is the resistance in the churches to the feminist revolution.[4] The classic sociological account of the decline of religious observance in Britain was what was called 'secularisation theory'. The idea was that the Enlightenment and the Industrial Revolution gave birth to a new kind of consciousness that was inimical to religion and began the process of its dissolution. While there is clearly something in secularisation theory, Brown challenges many of its essential elements. One of the elements of the theory was that the Industrial Revolution alienated the working classes from Christianity. Brown dismisses that claim and shows that working class Britain was heavily involved in various forms of evangelical religion until fairly recently. The boom time in working class religiosity in Britain was the mid 1950s, of which the success of Billy Graham's crusades in 1954 was more a symptom than a cause. What Brown calls the background discourse of this period was the evangelical economy of salvation and it was a highly gendered discourse.

This is where I find his narrative convincing, because it

exactly mirrors my own theological experience. Traditional Christianity was based on very rigid gender roles. Women were subordinated to men as far as leadership went, but were viewed as spiritually superior to them and sent by God to restrain and civilise them. All of this was based on a particular reading of the Bible as well as on a particular stage of social evolution, and it still lies behind the nostalgia that characterises the debate about the family in Britain and the USA. When Christian feminists started challenging these stereotypes, traditionalists argued against them, claiming that changes in gender roles would undermine the whole biblical system and nothing would remain unchallenged. During the debate on the ordination of women, I remember arguing against the traditionalists on the grounds that they were exaggerating the effect that ordaining women would have. This was not a revolution, I argued, it was a tiny adjustment of the dial of history to accommodate changes in relationships between women and men. The ministry would not be affected by admitting women, it would only be widened slightly. Everything would go on as before, except that there would now be women wearing dog collars. We would get used to the change, as we did when women doctors arrived on the scene, and after a few months we would think nothing of it. Not so, argued the traditionalists: make this change and, in time, the whole edifice will fall. Historic Catholic Christianity is all of a piece, a minutely articulated whole; if you take one piece out of the structure, the whole thing will fall apart. If you question an element as central as this, you substitute human judgement for divinely revealed truth and the whole system will collapse like a stack of cards.

Though their motive was wrong, the prediction made by

the traditionalists is gradually coming true, and it is one of the main elements in Brown's revisionist theory of church decline. In a remarkably short period after 1963 the edifice started to crumble, except for a few defensive redoubts that still guard the old tradition with increasing desperation. What finished off Christianity in Britain, therefore, was not the slow creep of secularism, but the swift success of the women's movement. That is Brown's central claim. He is well aware of the way the experience of the United States appears to contradict his thesis, but his response is instructive:

The way of viewing religion and religious decline in Britain offered in this book should have wider applicability. It may help to explain the near contemporaneous secularisation of Norway, Sweden, Australia and perhaps New Zealand, and should help to account for the rapid secularisation of much of Catholic Europe since the 1970s. Critically, it may help to explain the North American anomaly. Throughout secularisation studies from the 1950s to the 1990s, the United States and Canada have seemed difficult to fit in the British model of religious decline. A supposedly obvious 'secular' society of the twentieth century has sustained high levels of church-going and church adherence. Debate on this has gripped American sociologists of religion for decades without apparent resolution. Perhaps the answer lies in seeing the same discursive challenge as Britain experienced *emerging* in North America in the 1960s, but then not *triumphing*. A discursive conflict is still under way in North America. The Moral Majority and the evangelical fight back has been sustained in public rhetoric in a way not seen in Europe. North American television nightly circulates the traditional evangelical narrative of conversionism . . . and a discursive battle has raged since the 1960s. Secular post-hippy culture of environmentalism, feminism and freedom for sexuality co-exists beside a still-vigorous evangelical rhetoric in which home and family, mother-hood and apple pie, are sustaining the protocols of gendered religious identity. Piety and femininity are still actively enthralled to each other, holding secularisation in check. In Foucaldian terms, North America may be experiencing an overlap of epistemes (of modernity and post-modernity).[5]

The fundamental issue in this debate is not whether you or I prefer the traditional evangelical version of gender identity to the post-modern feminist interpretation, but whether it is right to claim the traditional version as exclusively Christian. We all have preferences in life and sometimes we are more comfortable with the way things were than with the way things are. Some people like to be old fashioned, some people like to be absolutely *au courant*. Sometimes we even twist back on ourselves and establish a *retro-look*, in which we give a contemporary spin to a previous model, whether in clothing or furnishing. Post-modernism is so plural it can even find a place for yesterday or for last century in its design. Society is full of interesting survivals of this sort, including groups who exist to promote the restoration of various European monarchies. In Scotland there are groups that plan for the return of the House of Stuart to a renewed Scottish mon-archy. They gather from time to time in out-of-the-way buildings, dramatically swathed in coloured cloaks, to plan the return of the king from over the water, who, though a genetic descendant of the Stuarts, is probably an elderly Portuguese wine exporter. There is no harm in this. It's all part of the heritage industry and our endearing nostalgia for extinct cultures and their artefacts. The big question for the churches is whether they are so identified with the values of a previous culture that they are incapable of adapting to its successor. The culture wars of North America, in which Christianity is identified not only with a particular version of gender relationships, but with a hatred of sexual minorities and contemporary human freedoms, is a prospect that dismays Christians who are at ease in the new culture of post-modernity. Of course, one can prefer a particular culture without being blind to its defects. Every way of ordering society has its shadow side, and post-modernity is no exception. The issue is not whether it is imperfect, but whether any other way of ordering society, including the one associated with religious conservatism, would be significantly better. The fundamental question is whether it is right for Christianity to identify previous cultural arrangements exclusively with the mind of God. Human experience would suggest that out-of-date systems are no more likely to be perfect than up-to-date systems. The fact is that up-to-date is where most of us are, for better or for worse, and there is a lot to be said for accepting rather than running from the situation in which we find ourselves.

We now see the human struggle to discover meaning and value as an enterprise that produces many approaches, many answers, and we believe that there is something of value in that very variety. Geneticists talk about the phenomenon of 'hybrid-vigour' when different races inter-breed, and the same can be said of mixing cultures. More negatively, the presence of many systems is a good bulwark against the tendency to abuse that is found in societies where a single system dominates. Monopolies always become arrogant. The relativising effect of other accounts of the human adventure tempers the arrogance of single systems and moderates the endless contention in societies with two dominant systems. Voltaire understood this: '. . . if you have two religions in your land, the two will cut each other's throats; but if you have thirty religions, they will dwell in peace'.[6] Voltaire expresses the best value of post-modernity in that quotation. When authority, in religion as well as politics, is dispersed among many centres, it helps to neutralise the corrupting and oppressive effects of power. But there is an inevitable rear-guard action on the part of traditional centres of power. We see something of this going on in the political debate about the role of the European Union in the lives of its member states. And we see something of the same dynamic in the relationship between churches and other faith communities. The new ethic of pluralism is difficult for exclusive theological systems to deal with. If you have strongly internalised the belief that your team, whether ethnic or religious, is superior to all others, you will find contemporary multiculturalism difficult to cope with. It will be even more difficult if you believe that your system is exclusively true and no salvation beyond it is possible. Comfortable co-existence with neighbours who are on their way to damnation is an awkward feat to carry off.

There are many casualties of the culture wars in North America, such as the relationships within the family of a Presbyterian minister I heard about. John, a conscientious if unimaginative pastor of large suburban churches, was a characteristic product of early twentieth-century North American Protestantism. A gentle, liberal-minded man of deeply conservative instincts, he had three daughters, two of whom married ordained ministers, while the third married a wealthy stockbroker. Shortly after John's death, the wife of the stockbroker became a born-again Christian and announced to her mother that she knew that her father was in hell because he had never been converted and given his life to Jesus. Traditional Presbyterianism, apparently, just didn't have the fuel to get souls to heaven. Sick jokes like this one aside, the story illustrates the dilemma that faces Christianity today. There is much in the Christian tradition that can be wheeled in to support the ugly exclusivism of the rich sister's religion. There is plenty of stuff in our past that makes the sentencing of this gentle American pastor to eternal torment mild by comparison. When Callum Brown discussed the contrast between traditional evangelical Christianity and contemporary human experience he focused on the specific role of women, but he could have made the same point in a more general way. The real question at issue is not the consequence for any particular individual of holding to the classic evangelical economy of salvation, but the whole set of assumptions that undergirds it. When Christian traditionalists opposed the emancipation of women within the Church they intuitively understood that the real issue was the authority of the Bible and the religious claims that have been based upon it. If you believe that every word in the Bible is dictated by God, then you are going to have massive problems with contemporary society, particularly with the liberation of women.

Let me come at it from the other side for a moment: if you are a Christian who believes in the freedom of women to order their own destiny, within the normal limitations that define any human life, then you have already started to deconstruct the traditional view of the Bible. A contest has occurred and been resolved, whether you are consciously aware of it or not. The contest is between what you now believe to be the right of women to the same freedoms and opportunities as men and the traditional, biblical view of their status as intrinsically subordinate to men. As Brown reminded us, the classic Christian attitude to these matters set down a precise and unalterable set of gender identities. That is quite clear, so the choice is obvious. Brown suggests that, because people in Europe and (though perhaps less clearly) in North America have chosen to affirm and celebrate the right of women to embrace roles that were previously closed to them, they have simply abandoned Christianity *en masse* because they believe it to be fundamentally inconsistent with their new consciousness. For these people, the traditional Christian understanding of life is no longer plausible. It is as irrelevant to them as crinolines and stage coaches. It is true that a trickle of refugees from post-modern consciousness continues to seek asylum in traditional religious systems because they find a life of multiple choice difficult to sustain. Even here there is something unmistakably post-modern going on, however, because self-consciously choosing a life-style from a rack of earlier models is a very contemporary thing to do. Riding round London on a high bicycle with an old basket on the handlebars, wearing a carefully tailored three-piece suit and a brown trilby is an example of post-modern retro-chic, especially if you are on your way to a Latin High Mass at Brompton Oratory.

The question for Christianity is whether the options for choice are limited to the two I have described: either abandon Christianity, because it is so manifestly out of tune with what you consider to be the best values of contemporary culture; or cling to a version of Christianity that is profoundly antipathetic to the freedoms of post-modern society. Most people in our culture have already decided that Christianity is a kind of consciousness that is no longer possible for them, so they have simply abandoned it. Their opposition is fortified when they hear the most vocal group in Christianity today loudly denouncing the very values they have come to cherish. The representatives of traditional Christianity claim that the Bible presents us with a permanently valid way of understanding the universe and ordering human relations within it. Far from reflecting the science and ethics of a particular era of history, they assert that the Bible is fixed and unalterable truth, which no one is at liberty to alter. This is why you will sometimes hear the more tender-hearted among this group of conservative Christians say to homosexual people: we would, on the human level, love to be able to affirm your gay and lesbian relationships, but it is not up to us; God has firmly decreed what is right and what is wrong in this area and our response has to be obedience to that command, no matter how personally sympathetic we are to your situation and the lousy luck that has placed you in this horrible predicament.

Is that it, then? Christianity has already been pushed to the edges as an eccentric type of consciousness that is profoundly antipathetic to contemporary values: are we to witness its slow but inevitable death, apart from a few refugee encampments, here and there? Is there a third approach, which is not a middle way between belief and unbelief and is neither diluted fundamentalism nor watered-down scepticism? There is another group in the game, though whether they will be sent off the field is still an open question, since they tend to be despised by both the other groups as traitors. This group believes that it is possible to be Christian and post-modern, to be a member of a church and a supporter of feminism and the rights of sexual minorities, in spite of the witness of Christian tradition. It is a radical position, which has uncoupled Christianity from absolute claims about the status of the Bible and tradition. And the thing that broke the chain, as the traditionalists rightly foresaw, was the emancipation of women. Having embraced the ethical imperative of feminism, those of us who are members of this group came to realise that we now read the Bible as a human, not as a divine creation. The issue for those of us who find ourselves in this position is whether we can discover new ways of using the Christian tradition that will deepen our humanity, our care for the earth and for one another. That is the agenda I have set myself in this book.

My working assumption is that the discoveries we have made in our quest for meaning have all come from us, are *all* human constructs. Their existence is testimony to our extraordinary creativity as a species. We are constantly digging for meaning, searching for understanding. Later in this book I shall make use of one of the most influential texts of our era, Thomas Kuhn's *The Structure of Scientific Revolutions*. Kuhn argued that, in seeking to understand and interpret the world that lies before us, we have created habits of thought and practice that he called 'paradigms'. These are working systems of interpretation that endure until they are succeeded by systems that do the job better. Ptolemaic astronomy was succeeded by the Copernican system, which was succeeded by Newtonian physics; and so endlessly on. We are astoundingly fertile in our conceptions. There is unlikely to be a final, settled endgame which absolutely establishes everything in some kind of totalistic theory, because it is our nature to go on in our quest for understanding through time and space. It is important to remember that a wise humanity does not dismiss previous paradigms with contempt or scoff at them as primitive. They were valid interpretations of the world for their time, though they were later succeeded, usually after struggle and contention, by other points of view. If you accept the Kuhnian approach to meaning, then you find yourself in a state of permanent, but relaxed and expectant uncertainty. You don't make absolute claims for your present position, but you allow it to work for you as long as it can, till the next set of revolutionary insights replaces it.

I shall argue in this book that that is the best approach to the great religious narratives and systems that have been such a profound part of the human story. It is obvious that the astronomy of the creation narratives of Genesis no longer works for us, so it is just silly to cling to that ancient paradigm as a piece of descriptive science. It is inevitable that the religious narratives that have come down to us are framed in the science and social norms of their own day. Do we reject them totally for that reason, as many people appear, reasonably, to have done? Is Christianity to be abandoned because of its accidental historical framework, which includes an attitude to women that is profoundly at variance with our own best values today, or does it contain an enduring challenge that needs to be separated from its incidental context? Since I believe that the Christian account of meaning has to be separated from its historical packaging if it is to work for us today, I spend time in this book deconstructing important aspects of the Christian doctrinal tradition, such as original sin, incarnation and resurrection, but my ultimate intention is resoundingly positive. I am more interested in using the power of these great themes for our lives today, than in discarding the ancient containers that convey them to us.

I try to distinguish between the transient and the enduring elements of both the Hebrew and the Christian scriptures, and suggest that it is better to see them as good poetry than as bad science if they are to have meaning for us today. My aim is to craft from the Christian past a usable ethic for our own time. What I shall propose, however, is not a middle path between those who hold to the old beliefs and those who totally reject them; it will be a way of action. At the heart of Christianity there lies a moral challenge that is as pertinent today as it ever was. I shall argue that it is more important to follow the way of Jesus than to believe or disbelieve the traditional Christian claims about him. If I am right, then the real task for Christianity today is the challenge not to go on interpreting the world in the old way, but to start disturbing it with renewed power.

CHAPTER TWO

Burning Bright

In *Alice's Adventures in Wonderland*, one of Lewis Carroll's droller inventions is the Cheshire Cat that slowly disappears, starting with the tail and ending with the smile, which remains suspended in the air for some time after the rest of the cat has gone. The vanishing cat is an apt metaphor for the history of God in our era. One of the indisputable facts of our time is the gradual reduction of God's role in the specific management of the world: as our knowledge of the universe increases, God's function shrinks until little is left except a feeling of absence or a vague sense of bereavement. It is true that generalised belief in God persists widely, but it has lost much of the explanatory clarity it once had. Even conservative believers are more careful about the claims they make. Some reject the explanations of science and go on using God to fill up gaps in their knowledge of the universe, but for most people in Western society God's role is now problematic. There may be a persistent sense that there is some mysterious power behind the origin of the universe, but there is little hard confidence about what God is or does, apart from being a convenient place to stop the endless explanatory regress that attempts to account for things. Indeed, the explanatory side of religion, which was once so dominant, now seems to be its most fragile element.

What most characterises us as humans is our consciousness, our ability to think about ourselves. We were thrown into life with no procedural manual supplied, so we had to spend a lot of time trying to figure it out for ourselves, and supernatural religion was one of the first explanations we came up with. We experienced ourselves as dual creatures, strangely bifurcated into reason and sense, ideal and appetite, body and soul. Divided within ourselves, it is easy to understand how we projected our own dual nature onto the universe and divided it into a spiritual and a material realm, with the former controlling the latter. Nietzsche's version of this was to claim that the origin of religion lay in the way we experience these two realms in our dream life:

> *Misunderstanding of the Dream.* In the ages of crude primeval culture man believed that in dreams he got to know another real world; here is the origin of all metaphysics. Without the dream one would have found no occasion for a division of the world. The separation of body and soul, too, is related to the most ancient conception of the dream; also the assumption of a quasi-body of the soul, which is the origin of all belief in spirits and probably also of the belief in gods. 'The dead live on; for they appear to the living in dreams'; this inference went unchallenged for many thousands of years.[1]

Other guesses to account for the origin of religion have been offered. What we might describe as a generic account was offered by the Enlightenment philosopher of history, Giambattista Vico. His educated guess about the beginning of human community and the emergence of the supernatural account of meaning fixes on the move from forest to cave in the early development of humanity. The move from the uncertainty of the forest to the controllable environment of the cave created the conditions for the emergence of patriarchy and the family state. Vico saw the origins of religion in the cave dwellers' reaction to thunder and lightning, a guess that is backed up by primitive cave drawings. These elemental forces of nature were easily identified as the anger of mysterious agents of unpredictable power. They gave rise to the primitive religion of augury and appeasement, the basis for the cruelty that is intrinsic to many religious systems, however refined and developed they later become. These mysterious and unpredictable agents above us have to be placated, so intricate systems of divination and appeasement are developed to protect humans from their arbitrary whims. The priestly arts of augury and haruspication emerge; and they never quite leave human consciousness, as the continuing popularity of astrology and the abiding power of superstition attest.

More sophisticated and developed theistic religions assert that their faith is based on a true and final knowledge of God, no matter how misunderstood God may have been in the past. They are usually based on the claim that God was revealed in certain events that were subsequently recorded in a book that must be true because it was divinely inspired. Matthew Tindal, an eighteenth-century divine, mockingly described the circularity of this way of putting things. 'It's an odd jumble to prove the truth of a book by the truth of the doctrines it contains, and at the same time conclude those doctrines to be true because contained in that book.'[2] The frustrating thing about a lot of religious discourse is its inevitable circularity, like a dog chasing its tail. To change the image, arguing about God is like trying to pick up mercury with our fingers. It is the fascinating impossibility of it all that makes it so compelling.

Not everyone is fascinated, of course. There are people for whom the issue is permanently resolved. They either believe in God or they don't. In either case, they have resolved the question of God, one way or the other. The use of the verb 'resolved' suggests the result of a process of applied consideration, the end of an exploration or period of research into the matter that yields acceptable conclusions, either for or against the question. I suspect that it is rarely like that. Believers often describe faith as a gift, something they find themselves in possession of. Settled unbelief also seems to be a kind of gift, an attitude people find themselves holding without too much anguish about the matter. Even agnostics have a certain settled quality about them. They have settled for knowing that they do not know; but at least they have the certainty of knowing that there is no way of knowing whether there is a God. There are some of us who experience none of this consoling confidence of conviction, because both the possibility and the impossibility of God nibble at our souls – the phrase comes from Emily Dickinson's poem, 'This World is not Conclusion':

> This world is not conclusion.
> A Species stands beyond –
> Invisible, as Music –
> But positive, as Sound –
> It beckons, and it baffles –
> Philosophy – don't know –
> And through a Riddle, at the last –
> Sagacity, must go –
> To guess it, puzzles scholars –
> To gain it, Men have borne
> Contempt of Generations,
> And crucifixion, – shown –

> Faith slips – and laughs, and rallies –
> Blushes, if any see –
> Plucks at a twig of Evidence –
> And asks a Vane, the way –
> Much gesture from the Pulpit –
> Strong Hallelujahs roll –
> Narcotics cannot still the Tooth
> That nibbles at the soul –[3]

People who suffer from this condition of chronic uncertainty do not want to be negative in their dealings with those who adopt other approaches, but the fact that they place a heavy premium on personal honesty causes them concern at the many ways in which claims about God have been misused. The tone that people use in this discussion is important, so I want to find a voice that does not sound dismissive of the settled approaches I have touched on. Good people believe and do not believe that there is a God; and some other good people believe that it is impossible to know. Since I do not seem able to settle for any of these attitudes, let me cut directly to the question that concerns me.

We know that our planet is a tiny speck in a corner of a galaxy of billions of stars in a universe of billions of galaxies. Given the size of the universe, it is possible that the conditions that gave rise to life on our planet have been replicated elsewhere, but it is also possible that in all that unimaginable vastness, the mere thought of which so terrified Pascal, we are the only conscious creatures. It is possible that only on our planet, among a perfect infinity of possibilities, life has evolved to consciousness; so that only here, on this tiny dot, has the universe become conscious of itself and we have started thinking. The thing that bends the mind is the question: was there ever just nothing, and from that nothing did all this just spontaneously come forth? It is the existence of the universe, the being of Being and our ability to think about it, that is the tooth that nibbles at my soul. In some people, the questions have induced such anxiety and such a desperate need for answers to still the mind's vertigo, that we confront the odd spectacle of thinking creatures roasting each other alive over the status of their conjectures on the meaning of a universe that is intrinsically mysterious. The claim to absolute knowledge in this area has to be absurd. All claims to final knowledge of the meaning of things are cognitively dubious, though we might acknowledge that they can serve as comforts in a lonely universe. Today we believe in allowing people to hold absolute opinions, as long as they do not claim the right to torture and persecute others into holding them as well. Absolute systems, by definition, do not entertain the possibility of negotiating with other points of view. Historically, tolerance was forced on contending absolutists more by external force than by internal concession. It is worth remembering in our tolerant era that many of the conjectures from the past about the meaning of the universe have claimed for themselves the right to impose themselves on others. The paradox of our day is that we extend toleration to systems of belief that are themselves intrinsically intolerant, as a news story from 1998 confirmed.

It concerned two Sunday school teachers in a church in England who told their students, on the first anniversary of her tragic death, that Princess Diana was now in hell. One child, upset by the information, told his mother, who reported it to the press. In a radio interview the teachers claimed that Christianity taught that unrepentant sinners went to hell. Since Diana was an adulterer who had died suddenly, unprepared and unrepentant, it followed that she must be in hell. I was torn between admiration for their heroic disregard for public opinion, and horror at the cruelty of their belief system. However, the convictions they proclaimed would have been familiar to most Christians throughout history, who were taught that dying in unrepented sin guaranteed eternal punishment. This grisly doctrine was a consequence of one of the answers to the question about the meaning of the universe that humans have constructed. The system taught that this life is a mere prelude to a more important life beyond, and the way we live here, including the way we think, has eternal consequences. From the point of view of the topic of this chapter, it matters eternally how you answer the question about life's meaning; get it wrong, and you could find yourself in an eternity of torment.

It was this conviction about the fundamental and eternal consequences of holding the right answer to the question posed by life that led to the missionary expansion of Christianity. If you were persuaded that the answer to the question posed by life determined our eternal status after death, it would obviously have a profound effect on your attitude to other people, including people you would never meet. If you were a kindly person and you believed you had found the right answer to the meaning of life, you would want to share it with others, because it would rescue them from an eternity of torment beyond death. You might even be able to persuade yourself that the issues were so momentous for the people concerned that torturing them to accept the saving formula would be a virtuous act, for what are a few hours of torment in this life compared with an eternity of bliss in the life to come? Believers in absolute systems would see torture as a therapeutic intervention, like surgery, that was designed to save, not destroy, the soul.

Religions that make these absolute claims are often mutually exclusive. Even within Christianity there is claim and counter-claim about the status of different systems of belief. The logic goes something like this: only Christians can be saved; we know that this group is not really Christian, because it does not conform to the only true version of the faith; therefore those who cleave to this type of Christianity cannot be saved, unless they repent and conform henceforth to our system. The difficulty with absolute systems is finding some principle that might help us choose between them. How are we to discern between the rival claims? What makes discrimination impossible is that what we see is always and only the human end of the alleged revelatory transaction. The sacred texts that are claimed as evidence of the divine status of the faith are themselves human creations, and we know a great deal about their history. Nowadays, there are reckoned to be three ways of thinking about the status of sacred texts, described by theologians as *naïve realism*, *critical realism* and *non-realism*. The naïve realist takes the sacred texts literally and claims that God actually visited mountain tops and burning bushes and spoke human, recordable words to people in their own language. The non-realist would say that nothing was happening outside the minds of those who experienced the revelations, and what was going on was straightforward projection.

The position of the critical realist is less easy to define or describe. If we imagine the responses to the question as a semicircular dial, with non-realism at the extreme left and naïve realism at the extreme right, then critical realism would find itself in the centre, at a ninety-degree

angle to the base line of the semicircle. The point of
this illustration is to suggest that, as with all of these
things, there are degrees of difference within all the broad
categories. Critical realism would hold that there is that
which we call God, but that it is encountered by humans
in ways that are relative to their place in the universe. In
other words, for the critical realist, religious experience *is*
an experience of the Real, but it is always mediated in forms
that are not necessarily 'real' in the hard empirical sense.
This position is called 'critical' realism precisely because
it believes that it is necessary to put religious claims to
careful examination and interpretation. This is how John
Hick puts it: 'Religious experience occurs in many different
forms, and the critical realist interpretation enables us to
see how these may nevertheless be different authentic
responses to the Real. But they may also not be. They
may instead be human self-delusion. Or they may be a
mixture of both. And so a critical stance in relation to them
is essential.'[4] Then he goes on to make an important point:
'. . . the forms taken by religious experience are provided
by the conceptual equipment of the experiencer'. He
quotes Thomas Aquinas: 'Things known are in the knower
according to the mode of the knower.' Hick comments:

> this fundamental epistemological principle has a wider
> application than Aquinas himself intended. For the mode of
> the knower has been differently formed within the various
> religious traditions, producing our different awarenesses
> of the divine. The fourteenth century Sufi Al-Junayd
> expressed the same principle more poetically when he
> said, 'The colour of water is that of its container'; and
> Al-'Arabi later added, 'If one knew Junayd's saying, "The
> water takes its colour from the vessel containing it", he
> would not interfere with other men's beliefs, but would

perceive God in every form of belief.' For the different traditions are the containers that give its recognisable colour to human awareness of the Transcendent.[5]

No matter which position we adopt on the question of the reality of God, there is a difficulty that affects them all. There is a problem in philosophy called the paradox of appearance: is there a world out there independent of our perception of it? Common sense would suggest to us that there is; but the fact remains that we can only know that world through our perception of it. It is our mind, the recording device between our ears, that puts us in touch with what is out there and plays it back for us. There is no view from anywhere that can establish the world's independent existence for us *apart* from our perception of it. So there is a sense in which it is true to say that it is our mind that calls the world into being for us, along with everything else, including God. There is no satisfactory way out of this paradox; all the solutions we offer turn out to be versions of the same old problem. So, if there is God and a world out there, we can only know them, understand them, be in touch with them, through the agency of our own perceptions. This promotes in me neither despair at ever being able to get hold of anything outside my own head, nor the kind of immobilising scepticism that believes nothing can be said accurately about anything. What it does compel me to accept is the powerful creativity of human consciousness in the act of knowing anything, including God. This has to rule out the possibility of naïve realism, because it fails to take into account the contribution we unavoidably make to any kind of encounter with reality.

As far as the status of God is concerned, I find the needle on my own dial trembles midway between non-realism

(God is a human invention) and critical realism (there is a mystery out there, but we are inextricably involved in its interpretation and never get it with complete purity). On the one hand, I cannot return to an understanding of religious claims that is pre-critical; on the other hand, I am not quite prepared to reduce the whole of religious experience to human projection, though much of it clearly is. I am haunted by the strangeness of the universe, by its sacredness as well as by its obviousness. I am not prepared to rule out the possibility of experiences of a reality beyond the three-dimensional reality that I mainly encounter. And from time to time I have crossed strange, invisible thresholds into other dimensions of reality. Another way to put this is to say that I am troubled by the enigma of the universe and the possibility of God. I find myself encountered by a mysterious depth in life that religions call the sacred, the beyond or the other.

If we accept, if only for the sake of argument, that all religious systems and all language about the mystery we call God are, as far as we are concerned, fixed inescapably on the human side of the equation, so that we can only see and be in touch with the human effect and never the allegedly divine cause; and if we accept, if only for the sake of argument, that if there is that which we call God we can only be in touch with it through our own life and the life of the universe in which we are set; then one way to use the great guesses about God, the religious narratives and traditions, is to give them human meanings in order to see what they can teach us, what discoveries we might make through them and what guidance we might derive from them. The great question of the meaning of Being can then be allowed to overwhelm us with wonder in the presence of life itself. This is close to what believers call worship, acknowledging the worth of the mystery of Being, the extraordinary fact of the universe and of our place in it.

Thinking about the sun, the vast thermonuclear reactor in space whose unbelievable heat makes life possible on earth, is a good place to start this process of contemplation. To us the sun appears to be the largest and brightest of the stars, but it is actually the smallest and faintest. The illusion arises because of its comparative nearness – it is only 93 million miles away, while the next nearest star is nearly 300,000 times as far away, more than four light years. To get some idea of how far that is, consider that light traverses the 93 million miles from the sun to earth in only eight and half minutes. In four light years, it travels more than twenty trillion miles. The sun is a dwarf star, lying in a region of our galaxy, the Milky Way. Our galaxy contains about a hundred billion stars, ranging in mass from a tiny proportion of the mass of the sun to a hundred times the mass of the sun. And that is only our galaxy. There are many billions of galaxies in the observable universe. Our planet earth is a puny object in a violent, unbelievably vast and expanding universe, yet it has remained hospitable to life for at least three and a half billion years. Our very existence is a consequence of the stability of the sun, which has been burning long enough to allow life to evolve and flourish on our planet. Recently scientists caught a glimpse of the violence of that great burning star that makes our life possible. They detected a shock-wave on the sun and they mapped great tornadoes whipping round it at more than 100,000 miles per hour. It is that violent and blazing star whose light and heat come to us from 93 million miles away that makes it possible for us to sit comfortably in our homes thinking about it all. And that act of thought is almost as great a miracle as the universe. We are a sub-microscopic dot in a tiny corner of a small galaxy in a universe containing billions of galaxies, but in us the universe has become conscious, has started thinking about itself. The sun is not thinking about itself as it burns; the universe is not thinking about, is not conscious of itself as it explodes through space; but we are. Something is going on in us that is as wonderful and extraordinary as the universe itself.

In an engaging book written in 1995, Don Cupitt suggested that we should use the sun as a moral example.[6] Rather than living frightened and cautious lives, we should burn out extravagantly, giving warmth and joy to others. There is something in the universe that calls us to recklessness and extravagance. We see it in the work of great artists and composers, in great explorers and scholars, in great social reformers. A burning passion kindles them into life, into thought, into heroic achievement, into poetry and art, into love and compassion, into laughter and daring. We could let ourselves be ignited by the same recklessness that lies at the heart of the universe, challenging us to live adventurously, not to be held back by our fears and limitations, but to burn with joy that we are rather than that we are not. Meditating on the wonder of Being challenges us to live up to the measure of the universe and the mystery that called it into explosive existence. It would be hypocrisy to open our hearts and minds to the vastness of the universe and the heroic possibilities of human nature, if we allowed ourselves to become narrow and mean-spirited and closed our hearts towards our neighbours. Meditation on the majestic energy of the universe should increase our love for humanity, should widen, not narrow, our hearts.

The extravagance of the universe could be used as one of the keys to daring and creative living. The wonder of it impels us to give ourselves to great themes and possibilities, even to the possibility of God, which is a coded way of talking about the obligation we feel to do something with the one life we have been given. That is why we all mourn a wasted life or the wasted moments in our own life. The best of the Christian vision is the idea that we are important and that we should love one another before we die. It is a vision that won't leave some of us alone; and it continues to draw wonder and the troubled passion of faith from us. But the nature of that faith has changed. It is now faith in life and the intention to live it creatively and generously. There has been much in Christianity that has been damaging to humanity; too often it has allowed itself to become the vehicle of intolerance and hatred. But deep within it there lies a dynamic pity for those whose lives are stunted by the cruelty and indifference of the powerful. To release the revolutionary power of that pity into the world is the purpose of this book. It will fail if it is read simply as another imposition of guilt on people, however purged of supernatural fear it has become. No one *has* to follow the Christian path and this book certainly won't persuade you that you must. But you might just fall into it from sheer joy at its possibilities. Recently, someone sent me four lines of anonymous verse. They are all the justification I need:

Cease wretch to mourn to weep –
Sip up the sun.
We dance along death's icy rim,
But is the dance less fun?

CHAPTER THREE

Where all the Ladders Start

In the previous chapter I skated rapidly over the subject of revelation as a powerful source of religious claims. I now want to explore the subject more carefully and suggest a way in which we can give it a human use. A useful distinction used to be made between *natural theology* and *revealed theology*. The best way to work with the distinction is to think of an example, such as a house in the woods. You are out walking in a wood, when you come to a clearing in the midst of which there is a cottage. It is clearly an inhabited dwelling, because everything is in good order. There are curtains in the windows, a fire is burning in the grate of the parlour and a large room at the back is comfortably littered with books and papers. The whole place testifies to the personality of the owner, though he or she is not present. Using common sense and a flair for detective work, you build up a picture of the proprietor from the evidence that lies all around you. A pipe-rack on the mantelpiece suggests to you that the owner is likely to be a man. The hundreds of books that cram the cottage suggest a reader, a person of learning. The pictures on the wall and the careful attention to colour and design in the furnishings and decoration suggest someone for whom beauty and comfort are important. In this way, in the absence of the owner, using your natural reason, you build up a picture of him. You have, in fact, engaged in a piece of natural theology, deducing from evidence presented to

your senses the existence of, and something of the character of, the absentee owner. Arguments for the existence of
God used to follow that kind of procedure, Paley's watch
being one of the most famous of the versions offered, in
which the finder of a watch inferred from its presence on
the beach the existence of a watch-maker. Most of the
arguments from design were worked out before Darwin
discovered the unimaginably long aeons of time required
for the adaptation of species to their environment, and few
people offer them as serious arguments today, but they do
illustrate the distinction I am trying to explain.

It was held that, by our natural reason alone, we could
infer or deduce the existence of God from the evidence
our senses gave us of an order that required a creator, a
level of design that spoke of a designer and the presence
in our breasts of a conscience that pointed to the existence
of a moral structure to the universe. From all of that a
theoretical picture of God as an absentee creator was built.
However, there is something unsatisfying about a purely
hypothetical cottage owner. We long for him to stride out
of the forest and make himself known to us, invite us in
for tea, and charm us with his conversation and wisdom.
But we cannot be in control of that event; we can only
be alert to its possibility, and open to it when it occurs,
when the revelation finally takes place. *Revealed theology*,
therefore, is that knowledge of God that comes to us from
outside ourselves, from God, from beyond, and it tells us
things about God that we could not deduce for ourselves.
Revelations usually come through inspired individuals who
are recognised as having been with God; and these sacred
individuals either create, or there is created round them,
writings that record the details of their disclosures. *Revealed*
theology becomes the study of this body of material, and

it is usually approached with greater reverence and care than *natural* theology, because it is held to be sacred in itself. Sometimes this reverence is expressed liturgically as when, for example, the Book of the Gospels is carried in procession and is incensed and kissed during services in Church; or when devout Moslems turn towards Mecca in their prayers, since it was the place of revelation to the Prophet and is, therefore, sacred in itself.

The difficulty with the traditional distinction between natural and revealed theology is that no qualitative difference actually exists between the two sources of theological data, apart from the particular honour that has been accorded to the allegedly revealed elements. Even if we think there is something mysterious about the universe, and that it conveys some sense of latency or hidden presence, we have to admit that *everything* we know about it comes to us through, and is recorded by, our senses. We may be watching a person praying in church who is in deep communion with the invisible presence of her God, but all that is available to us is the human, this-worldly side of that transaction. We can only hear the sound of one hand clapping, as it were, see the person on her knees, rapt in devotion, not the presence she is focused upon. This need not necessarily imply the non-existence of the invisible presence that is beyond discernment by our senses; it *does* imply that we only have access to the bit that lies on this side of the interaction. Everything that is said or written about our relationship with the divine is inescapably human, made by us. The frustrating thing about this situation is that it usually leads to a futile conflict between those who believe in the transcendent origins of revelation and those who see it as a human activity of projection. Those who believe in revelation assert that it has come to them directly from God; those who believe that all religious claims can be explained in a naturalistic way dismiss their claim. What I want to suggest is that neither approach is really subtle enough to help us engage with the mystery of discovery that, in theological shorthand, we call revelation. Moreover, the natural way of accounting for revelation need not be reductive; it may, in fact, increase our amazement at the mystery of its creativity.

> Yet nature is made better by no mean,
> But nature makes that mean: so o'er that art,
> Which, you say, adds to nature, is an art
> That nature makes . . . The art itself is nature.[1]

I would like to propose that we replace the distinction between natural and revealed theology with a new distinction, between what I would like to call mental theology and imaginative theology. We begin by acknowledging that theology is a human activity, something *we* do, but we also acknowledge that it is done in different ways, rather like the distinction between right and left brain thinking. However we put it, we begin by recognising that all these mysterious discoveries come from us, are part of the extraordinary reality of human nature and its gift of consciousness. Our forebears described these mysteries in one way; we think about them in another way. What is common is the experience; what differs is the framework or template we create in order to express it. The reference frame of the biblical writers was a three-tier flat universe, with heaven above, earth in the middle and hell or the underworld literally beneath us. That is why there is all that spatial language in scripture about God being above us, and why when the hymn writers wanted to express something of the shock and newness of Jesus they said *'he came down to earth from heaven'*. We take that language metaphorically today. I am not absolutely convinced that the original authors did not also understand it metaphorically in their day, but it is now a cause of some confusion for us. The New Testament scholar Marcus Borg has said that one of the problems for theology today is that some people insist on historicising or literalising what were always meant to be metaphors, thereby robbing us of a powerful and permanent way of using the biblical material.[2] I can profitably use the metaphor of descent and ascent to describe the significance of Jesus; but if you insist that I take it literally, whatever you think you mean by that, then you deprive me of any valid and creative use of the biblical material. If we can move away from theology for a moment and look at another, related field of inspiration we might get a better understanding of the kind of distinction I am trying to make here.

When W.B. Yeats was an old man he thought that he had lost the gift of poetry. He brooded on the fact that, when younger, the images of inspiration, what he called his circus animals, had come to him unbidden from outside himself, by revelation, as it were; but now they seemed to have deserted him.

> I sought a theme and sought for it in vain,
> I sought it daily for six weeks or so.
> Maybe at last being but a broken man
> I must be satisfied with my heart, although
> Winter and summer till old age began
> My circus animals were all on show[3]

A new biography claims that many of Yeats' inspirations

came from his fascination with the occult. Yeats was 51 when he married George Hyde-Lees on 20 October 1917; his new wife was 21. It was a complex relationship, and there is plenty of evidence that Yeats was in love with someone else at the time. What cemented the relationship, at any rate during its early years, was George's facility for automatic writing. This fascinated Yeats; indeed, Brenda Maddox, author of *George's Ghosts*, the biography in question, suggests that his young wife contrived the arrangement, probably subconsciously, in order to capture her husband's interest, and that she continued to use it to direct the relationship, particularly in their sex life. After all, a 51 year old man, just married, probably needs prompting to embark upon fatherhood, and what better coach could there be for someone who was fascinated by and passionately believed in the occult than a friendly ghost? But George's ghosts provided more than sexual encouragement and advice on domestic arrangements; they provided powerful images that went into some of Yeats' most famous poems. Here is a passage from Maddox's fascinating book.[4]

In January 1919 Yeats completed what is probably the best-known poem of his later years, 'The Second Coming'. Incorporating the symbols he had been receiving through the Script [*the automatic writing his wife was doing at his request*] since his marriage, it could not have been more timely.

Europe was reeling from the effects of the war. From Russia Bolshevism cast its shadow over the old patterns of work. War had broken out between the sexes. Ireland was on the brink of rebellion and within Irish society the Protestant Ascendancy had lost its grip. The old order was dead. Yeats' poem encompassed it all:

Turning and turning in the widening gyre
The falcon cannot hear the falconer;
Things fall apart; the centre cannot hold;
Mere anarchy is loosed upon the world,
The blood-dimmed tide is loosed, and everywhere
The ceremony of innocence is drowned;
The best lack all conviction, while the worst
Are full of passionate intensity.

Maddox points out that this extraordinary poem is strong enough to accommodate all the meanings that have been read into it: historical, political, religious and scientific. Then she goes on to offer what she calls an obstetrical interpretation. I quote it here, not necessarily because I agree with it, but because it shows how revelatory texts are open to many interpretations and become larger than their original meaning or intention.

His personal life, with its newly established order, was menaced by the 'shape with lion body and the head of a man' advancing towards him in George's expanding belly. Very soon, after a burst of water and blood, he would be 'vexed to nightmare by a rocking cradle', deprived of the total attention of his wife on whom he had come to depend, torn by primitive jealousies he had long fought to bury and disturbed by squalling noise when he needed absolute silence for writing poetry. After the unstoppable beast's arrival, the one certain thing is that his life will never be the same again.

The Second Coming! Hardly are those words out
When a vast image out of *Spiritus Mundi*
Troubles my sight: somewhere in the sands of the desert
A shape with lion body and the head of a man,
A gaze blank and pitiless as the sun,

Is moving its slow thighs, while all about it
Reel shadows of the indignant desert birds.
The darkness drops again; but now I know
That twenty centuries of stony sleep
Were vexed to nightmare by a rocking cradle
And what rough beast, its hour come round at last,
Slouches towards Bethlehem to be born?

The main point here is not the cogency of any particular piece of Yeatsian interpretation, but the fact that Yeats, at this stage in his career, would have claimed that his poetic symbols, his inspiration, came from another world, a realm outside himself, 'The Second Coming' being a potent example of that revelatory process. But, in 'The Circus Animals' Desertion', he is an old man, unable to compose, his circus animals all on strike, refusing to visit him. Gradually, he realises that it was, all along, his own heart that was the source of his inspiration, and not some exalted sphere beyond himself. So he realises he must get back inside himself, back to where all the ladders of effort and inspiration start, like someone struggling to lift himself out of a slum. The poem ends:

. . . now that my ladder's gone,
I must lie down where all the ladders start
In the foul rag and bone shop of the heart.[5]

I think Yeats' experience offers us a way of understanding how inspiration or revelation really works, no matter what frame of reference we use to describe it, whether supernatural or occult. All the ladders start in the human heart: we generate the material; we create the images; the art comes through us or, to be more precise, through people of genius, inspired individuals. Using that as an approach, I want to look at a passage from the Acts of the Apostles in the Christian scriptures that will help us think about the meaning and processes of revelation, of those new discoveries we go on making about our own nature and the nature of the universe.

[10:1] In Caesarea there was a man named Cornelius, a centurion of the Italian Cohort, as it was called. [2] He was a devout man who feared God with all his household; he gave alms generously to the people and prayed constantly to God. [3] One afternoon at about three o'clock he had a vision in which he clearly saw an angel of God coming in and saying to him, 'Cornelius.' [4] He stared at him in terror and said, 'What is it, Lord?' He answered, 'Your prayers and your alms have ascended as a memorial before God. [5] Now send men to Joppa for a certain Simon who is called Peter; [6] he is lodging with Simon, a tanner, whose house is by the seaside.' [7] When the angel who spoke to him had left, he called two of his slaves and a devout soldier from the ranks of those who served him, [8] and after telling them everything, he sent them to Joppa.

[9] About noon the next day, as they were on their journey and approaching the city, Peter went up on the roof to pray. [10] He became hungry and wanted something to eat; and while it was being prepared, he fell into a trance. [11] He saw the heaven opened and something like a large sheet coming down, being lowered to the ground by its four corners. [12] In it were all kinds of four-footed creatures and reptiles and birds of the air. [13] Then he heard a voice saying, 'Get up, Peter; kill and eat.' [14] But Peter said, 'By no means, Lord; for I have never eaten anything that is profane or unclean.' [15] The voice said to him again, a second time, 'What God has made clean, you must not call profane.' [16] This happened three times, and the thing was suddenly taken up to heaven.

Remembering where all the ladders start, in the foul rag and bone shop of the heart, how can we interpret this interesting story? The admission of the gentiles to the Jesus movement was clearly the most contentious issue in the life of the young community. James of Jerusalem, the brother of Jesus, was the conservative of the movement, who resisted any liberalising of the requirements of the Jewish Law for gentile converts. The young church was a messianic movement within Judaism, a tendency, a sect; but at this stage it had no pretensions to replace or go beyond Judaism, which the admission of the gentiles would effect. The new and zealous convert to the movement, still deeply mistrusted by its leadership, was the radical Paul, who believed that the new revelation of God that had come through Jesus had superseded the Jewish Law. And Peter, like many leaders anxious to preserve institutional unity, was caught in the middle. We can imagine the turmoil in his mind, which even invaded his dreams. The fascinating thing about the dream of the sailcloth let down from heaven, containing creatures forbidden to a Jew, was that it represented a struggle in Peter's understanding of the authority of scripture, a subject that still torments believers today. God had already forbidden the very creatures Peter was now being commanded to eat. Peter's dilemma is that he has a hunch God is now inviting him to change his mind; God is revising God! Is scripture a word for all time or can our interpretation of it be revised to allow us to respond to new challenges and conditions? That is a very modern dilemma, but it was Peter's dilemma at Joppa. Again, we need not leave Peter's heart to account for the struggle and its resolution: that's where all the ladders start. We know that Peter resolved the question, at any rate for the time being, when Cornelius came knocking on the door asking for baptism. And that, too, fits the dynamic of human revelation. We struggle intellectually or psychologically with an abstract issue: can women be ordained? should gay and lesbian people be allowed the blessing of the Church for their relationships? At this stage it is a theoretical issue in our own hearts and heads, but soon it becomes a person knocking at the door like Cornelius, and we are called out of the refuge of abstraction to confront real human beings who are being victimised by those same abstractions. That has certainly been my own experience. What begins as abstract theorising, almost as an intellectual game, soon becomes flesh and blood that makes its challenge directly and will not let me escape into theory. Your theory, this abstraction you struggle with, is actually about *me*, and it is causing me to suffer. Your theology *hurts* me, gets me beaten up, sometimes killed: think about it! Peter certainly thought about it, when confronted by Cornelius, but we know that he was not really converted, not really turned round inside, because he equivocated on a number of occasions, later on. Like many leaders, he wanted to keep his options, or his avenues, open to both sides of the issue.

From our point of view, the thing to notice is that all of this is going on inside us all the time. We can all testify to moments of conversion, moments when the scales fell from our eyes and we *saw*, for the first time, how racist or sexist or homophobic we had been. We did not really admit it to ourselves, of course, but it showed itself in all sorts of ways, usually by our use of language, by the throw-away remark that's meant to be funny but betrays deep prejudice or fear. When the moment of conversion comes, the moment we see what has been going on inside us, we use the language of revelation, the language of disclosure. And what it points to is the extraordinary subtlety and creativity of the human heart. If we stop trying to establish the independent existence of a supernatural realm that overwhelms us from outside, we are left with the profound fact of the depth and richness of our own unconscious from which insights and challenges emerge into our minds. The revelations of our religious imagination are among the most powerful of our creations. To acknowledge, perhaps for the first time, how they really work, need not empty them of their power. Just when we think all the ladders between heaven and earth have fallen down we discover that our own heart, all along, has been the source of our greatest insights. That's where all the ladders start.

CHAPTER FOUR

Cracking the Code

I have already mentioned Thomas Kuhn's essay *The Structure of Scientific Revolutions*.[1] Kuhn was a theoretical physicist at Harvard in 1947 when he was asked by the university president to teach a course on science to humanities students. While trying to reconcile Aristotle's physics with Newtonian thinking, it suddenly occurred to him that Aristotle's ideas were not 'bad Newton' but different ways of looking at the same thing.[2] Fifteen years after this epiphany, he articulated his ideas in his famous essay. In his ground-breaking work, Kuhn argued against the common view of science as the steady and incremental accumulation of observation, data, discoveries and inventions. Instead, he argued that the history of science is characterised by periods of peaceful and normal research punctuated by epochs of crisis and transformation. He called these crises 'scientific revolutions'. What Kuhn called 'normal' science begins when a community of scientists agrees about the nature of the basic entities they are talking about. They operate within a constellation of basic agreements which he called a 'paradigm'. 'Paradigms are essentially scientific theories or ways of looking at the world that fulfil two requirements: they must be "sufficiently unprecedented to attract an enduring group of adherents away from competing modes of scientific activity", and they must be "sufficiently open-ended to leave all sorts of problems for the redefined group of practitioners to resolve".'[3]

These paradigms are not permanent and unalterable descriptions of reality. They work as long as they work or until they are challenged by anomalies they cannot explain. It is the persistence of unexplained anomalies that precipitates a scientific crisis. Sometimes the current paradigm can be made to solve the problem. Sometimes no solution can be found and the problem is put on hold till a solution comes along. But sometimes a new paradigm emerges that replaces the old one, by providing better solutions to current difficulties, and so the process continues. Crucially, the breakdown of old paradigms and the emergence of new ones is often assisted by social forces. Kuhn used the debate over Copernicus' ideas in the sixteenth century as an example. While it is true that there was an increasing recognition of the discrepancy between what was then known about nature and the received Ptolemaic account of astronomy, the social need for calendar reform as well as the pressures of the emerging Renaissance contributed to the breakdown of the received paradigm and the acceptance of the new Copernican one.[4] However, it would not be accurate to say that the Ptolemaic paradigm was 'bad Copernicus'. It was a way of looking at the universe that no longer worked, as would later be the case with its successor, the Newtonian, mechanistic paradigm which, in turn, would be succeeded by the quantum paradigm. The current quantum paradigm no longer supplies satisfactory answers to certain anomalies discovered at the sub-atomic level, and a more complete paradigm will probably emerge. Undoubtedly, the new paradigm will be succeeded by another that does the job better, until it is eventually succeeded by one that we have not even begun to think about.

The important things to notice about Kuhn's essay is

that its central discovery can be applied not only to science, but to human knowledge in general. Significantly, it makes the notion of 'truth' contingent upon who and where and what we are. It does not seem to be the case that there is an absolute objective 'truth' about the universe out there waiting for us to happen upon, the way we might find a lost treasure in a sunken galleon. What seems to occur is that a point of view works for us, answers our questions, helps us to operate in life, so we use it until it no longer does the job it was designed for. We come to realise that our viewpoints were not pieces of concrete truth that we discovered and logged permanently into our minds; they were practical ways of dealing with what lay before us, problem-solving devices. And when better ways of doing and explaining things came along, we transferred our loyalties to them.

This notion that there is no fixed truth out there is extremely difficult for many people to accept. Their anxiety may have something to do with the normal human resistance to change and the over-turning of perceptions we have become comfortable with; but it probably has even more to do with an ancient attitude to reality that has been around at least since Plato. This is the conviction that there is an ideal, perfect, transcendent reality out there and that we should struggle to get our minds and wills to correspond to it. Kuhn's theory suggests that what we think of as 'true' at any one time is always related to where we are in history, so it is contingent, not fixed or absolute. The Platonic or dualistic view holds that there is a steady state of fixed value and truth somewhere, which in our present situation we only catch glimpses of, but which we must constantly struggle towards. Kuhn's epiphany challenges this kind of static mysticism. Malcolm Gladwell said of Kuhn's legacy that it 'will be remembered because he taught that the process of science was fundamentally human, that discoveries were the product not of some plodding, rational process, but of human ingenuity intermingled with politics and personality – that science was, in the end, a social process'.[5]

The claim that science, like everything else, is a social process is an important insight, because it challenges many of the ways in which the idea of truth has been handed down to us. Associated with the belief that truth has an objective solidity to which we must submit, there inevitably goes a system of authority. The most potent way to resolve the dilemmas of actual human experience and the painful disagreements they generate is to submit to agencies who already possess absolute knowledge. Our role then becomes one of receiving their revealed insights with humility and conscientiously obeying them. The history of philosophy would suggest that you are in one or other of these two groups. You are either some kind of dualist, who believes that there is an absolute perfection of truth out there to be sought and submitted to; or you are a pragmatist, someone who sees 'truth' as contingent upon where you are in history and as a way of talking about attitudes that work for you or of which you approve. The irony of the pragmatic approach to these matters, which I am trying to commend, is, of course, that it dare not claim absolute status for itself, for that is to go against its whole approach. It cannot make itself an exception to its own rule and declare that the provisionality of everything must now be accepted as an absolute rule. In time, it knows, that approach may have to be revised; but, for the time being, it seems the best way to do the things we have to do. For that reason, our adherence to it must be leavened with humour as well as irony, since these two things are closely related.[6] Pragmatic faith is happy to live in this unsettled state, because it is not in search of any absolute and irrefutable version of the truth; its sole ambition is to assist people to live more humanely and to limit the violence, including the spiritual and intellectual violence, they do to one another.

As a matter of fact, most people seem to *operate* in the pragmatic way, though they may claim to *believe* in an overarching theory of absolute truth. Let me suggest an example of this anomaly from the history of ethics. If we think about the status of women, for instance, we can see the matter from several different angles. If you are a dualist, who believes in the existence of absolute truth or value, you will probably believe in what are called 'objective standards', independent moral realities that stand on their own, irrespective of where *we* happen to be, and that it is our duty to correspond to them, by obeying them. But then anomalous things begin to happen. The objective standards may indeed still stand where they did, but *we* keep moving. The authoritative systems that mediate these fixed standards have conveniently provided documentary evidence to support their claims upon us. In the case of the status of women, as we have already noted, these authorities defined women in very precise and specific ways, usually as helpmates to men, with carefully circumscribed roles. This is certainly the case with the Bible. For instance, in Genesis 3.16 God says to Woman, after she has caused the Fall of Adam: 'I will greatly multiply your pain in childbearing; in pain you shall bring forth children, yet your desire shall be for your husband, and he shall rule over you.' Paul's version of this is found in I Corinthians 11.3ff.: 'I want you to understand that the head of every man is Christ, the head of a woman is her husband . . . for man was not made from woman, but woman from man. Neither was man created for woman, but woman for man.' You don't have to be Einstein to see how these prescriptions for women clearly had their origin in a specific historical context. At a certain stage of historical development biology will dictate an absolute destiny for most women; and we would expect societies to develop theories or explanatory myths to account for this fact. The Fall narrative in the Book of Genesis about the disobedience of Eve and her seduction of Adam is the classic explanatory myth within the Judaeo-Christian tradition. It offers an explanation for the laborious lives of women in primitive societies, as well as the pains of childbirth. The Fall narrative is what Kuhn would call a paradigm or a set of basic agreements that explain the way things are.

However, history is not static and one of the things it has clearly done in our culture is to deliver us from absolute biological necessity, so that we define ourselves today less by the pure processes of nature and more by the dynamics of human culture. As far as women are concerned, this means that they are increasingly liberated from biology to become agents of their own destiny, within the usual limits that define us all. In Kuhnian language, what we then begin to experience is a bad fit between the old paradigm and the new reality. The paradigm of biological necessity, or of objective gender standards, no longer answers the questions women are asking or solves the problems created by their new status. Since the old paradigm cannot resolve these anomalies, a revolution in our attitudes takes place and a new paradigm emerges. In the case of women today, there is a generally accepted agreement that they should no longer be totally bound by reproductive necessity and the gender roles that developed from it, and should be seen to be the equal of men.

It is obvious that this kind of paradigm shift in gender roles creates difficulties for groups who refuse to accept the historically contingent nature of truth claims or of so-called objective moral standards, particularly as they relate to men and women. The chances are that if you adhere to one of these traditional systems you will be experiencing considerable unease today because, while you have probably accepted many aspects of the new paradigm, your belief system or underlying theory of life is probably diametrically opposed to the new reality. The real dilemma for Christians who operate comfortably within post-modern society is how they are to use and understand traditional religious language today. At the heart of the difficulty is a philosophical conundrum called the problem of correspondence. Most of us, when we use language, implicitly believe that our words correspond to external realities, so that the word 'bread' is matched in some sense to the substance that satisfies our hunger and without which we would die. But a moment's thought will demonstrate how arbitrary and strange language is. Things are not what we say they are. The word bread is not itself eatable, though it points to or signifies a substance that is. One way to understand language, therefore, is as a sort of signalling system by which we give names to external objects. My baby son looks up at me and says 'Dada' and I am thrilled, because he has spoken his first word, made his first act of verbal identification. And while the word Dada is arbitrary, and some other sound would serve as well, it does make the link, and establishes the correspondence desired.

At this level, things are reasonably simple, but the plot begins to thicken. You could say that for the simple purpose of connective identification, the arbitrary naming of people and objects is straightforward and does its job well. But humans go on to use language to do much more than describe or signify. This is where the problem of correspondence starts. For instance, if I say, 'sodomy is sinful', I am clearly using language in a much more complicated way than when I say 'your name is John'. To unpack the meaning of the statement, 'sodomy is sinful', I have to start defining or explaining the terms. The first term, sodomy, is comparatively simple and is not particularly value-laden. When we come to the word 'sinful', however, we move into a more complicated word game in which agreement is not so easy to find. We would begin by defining 'sin', which could only be done by a careful consideration of the context in which the word arose. Having defined sin as an action that was held by a particular community to be against the commandment of its God, we would go on to identify the statement 'sodomy is sinful' as a belief held by a group of people in a particular context. In other words, we are saying that this set of words does not have an absolute and for-everyone kind of meaning, but only a meaning that corresponds to a particular context.

When you start thinking about it at any depth, language becomes much more elusive than we might at first think and the difficulty is particularly acute in religion. It is easy enough to offer a descriptive use of religious language by researching the various faiths in the world and saying what they believe. Religions do much more than this. They claim that their beliefs correspond to reality in some profound sense and reflect the values of an eternal world. This is particularly true of Christianity, which is the most dogmatic of the religions, using 'religion' here to refer to a system of belief that is held to correspond to eternal reality. Christianity claims to be putting us in touch with truth from another world that has an absolute claim upon us. The problem is that we have no way of getting independent verification of the eternal side of these claims. What can we accept as objectively true? How do we know that there is anything to which this language corresponds? People deal with these questions in different ways. Some probably aren't aware that there is a problem, so they are in the position I have already described as naïve realism, which believes that everything their religion says about anything exactly corresponds to reality in heaven and on earth. Others are aware of the problem, but they break out of the circle by *choosing to believe* in the claims made by their religion *as though they exactly corresponded to reality*. They say that, since we cannot get ourselves out of the correspondence problem and demonstrate the reality of the other side, we either reject its existence altogether or trust that religion puts us genuinely in touch with it through revelation, which is the direct action of God upon our minds and hearts.

I would like to suggest a different approach, which neither assumes nor attempts to establish the reality of the other world to which religious language claims to correspond. It is the impossibility of proving this correspondence that has created the crisis in Christianity for many people today. They cannot fit Christianity into their heads if it is taken as a set of claims about ancient miracles that are meant to correspond to historical fact. Nevertheless, they are haunted by some of the values of Christianity and would like to be associated with it in a way that did not violate their moral and intellectual integrity. This is exactly my own position. I have asked myself repeatedly in recent years whether I can still call myself a Christian, holding the faith in the way I now do. The answer to my question may be No and this book may conclusively demonstrate my departure from the faith I have given my life to. On other hand, and this is what I hope, it may offer a lifeline to people who, like me, want to remain members of the Christian community, but only if they can bring their minds, formed by the science and philosophy of the day, along with them. The approach I shall adopt is a version of philosophical pragmatism which holds that 'a belief is a habit of action'.[7] It will set out to show that holding Christian faith in a contemporary way commits us to a radical ethic, a habit of action, rather than to the holding of particular propositions in our heads. In addition to working out the consequences of that ethic, I shall attempt to break open the great Christian teachings in a way that makes them useful for our day. I shall use them as archetypes or myths, ways in which we share our own deepest wisdom and longing with each other. I shall try to show that a lot of religious language is best used as a kind of poetry that can illuminate our own existence and help us in the gaining of wisdom. When we understand religious language in this way we shall see that it bears close parallels with Kuhn's paradigm theory.

I have already suggested that religion is the result of our search for meaning. We look out on life and in on ourselves, and that act gives rise to religion, which is a way of connecting ourselves to the mystery of what is beyond ourselves, however we define it. That is why it is legitimate to think of atheism as a religious response, because it is a response to that ultimate concern, that final question we ask ourselves. What we call faith, of one sort

or another, is unavoidable here. Faith is our response to
that which we cannot establish with certainty. Atheists
express their attitude to these final or ultimate matters
in a God-denying faith, but there is no doubt of their
passionate concern over the matter. For Paul Tillich, the
only real atheism is lack of concern for the meaning of
our existence: 'Indifference toward the ultimate question
is the only imaginable form of atheism.'[8] Tillich defined
'ultimate concern' in this way: 'One is ultimately concerned
only about something to which one essentially belongs
and from which one is existentially separated.'[9] Because
of that potent experience of the combination of belonging
and separation, we create a language both to express our
ultimate concern and to connect ourselves with it. It is the
language of myth and symbol. Since our concern is over
the meaning of our own existence, the ultimate reality of
which we may doubt even as its possibility haunts us, we
develop a language of symbols with which to talk about it.
The word *symbol* is from the Greek for 'bringing together'
or making a connection. A national flag is an example of a
symbol that stands for or makes concrete the abstraction
of the nation. It becomes an emotionally potent way of
expressing national loyalty, as when athletes at the Olympic
Games wrap themselves in it after winning a gold medal,
or of expressing foreign hatred, as when it is burned by
the enemies of the nation.

In religious discourse, God is the ultimate symbol. This
little word connects us to all the questions we ask, and all
the longings we have, concerning ultimate meaning or its
absence. This is why the symbol 'God' is one of the most
ambiguous of human inventions. The Hebrews were so
aware of the unbridgeable gap between this symbol and
what it was intended to connect us with, that they were

afraid of using it and constantly pointed to its dangers. Since, by definition, God could not be what mortals said God was, they preferred to speak in circumlocutions or descriptive analogues rather than try to name God. This was the reason for their radical fear of idolatry, which is the identification of God with an object, either physical or conceptual. The classic text is from Exodus where the people grow frustrated with the God of Moses, who hides behind clouds on mountain tops. They want an accessible, portable God, and Aaron, the pliable religious functionary, obliges them: '"Take off the rings of gold which are in the ears of your wives, your sons, and your daughters, and bring them to me." So all the people took off the rings of gold which were in their ears, and brought them to Aaron. And he received the gold at their hand, and fashioned it with a graving tool, and made a molten calf; and they said: "These are your gods, O Israel, who brought you up out of the land of Egypt."'[10] Idolatry is always a greater danger to religion than atheism, because it identifies something we ourselves have created, something that is essentially an extension or projection of ourselves, with that which is beyond our knowing or creating. Even more significantly, the idolatrous tendency misunderstands the nature of symbols. Symbols may represent something beyond themselves; they may even, in some sense, connect us with it; but they are never the thing itself. We may appropriately show reverence and respect for the religious symbols we have created, because they link us to the real object of our worship; but we must not treat them as though they were the equivalent of the thing symbolised. If we fall into that trap, we confuse the finite with the ultimate, the medium with the mystery it delicately bears. That is why radical theism is close to atheism, and may

even be described as a form of practical atheism, because
it denies that the symbols of religion can ever be perfectly
identified with the mystery we call God. Those geniuses
of the spirit we call mystics know this intuitively and often
express it brutally. 'I pray to God to rid me of God,'
said German theologian and mystic Meister Eckhart. 'If
you meet the Buddha on the road, kill him,' goes a
commandment from the Eastern mystical tradition.

If we have to be careful about the claims we make for
religious symbols, we have to be doubly careful when
we come to the use of religious myths. Tillich defines
religious myths as 'symbols of faith combined in stories
about divine-human encounters'.[11] He points out that,
since the language of faith is the symbol, the expression
of faith is inextricably connected to myth. Myth is the way
we mediate our deepest experiences of God. He goes on
to point out that our myths have to be constantly criticised
and transcended, because of their very nature. He writes:
'[Myth] uses material from our ordinary experience. It puts
the stories of the gods into the framework of time and
space although it belongs to the nature of the ultimate
to be beyond time and space.'[12] The first criticism of the
divine myth takes us from polytheism to monotheism, but
even the notion of one God is unavoidably mythological,
because to speak of God at all is to draw God into time
and space. This is the same paradox we saw in discussing
the symbol 'God': to name God is already to limit God,
make God an entity. However, there is no escape from
the paradox of having to speak about that which is beyond
all our speaking. The same goes for our stories or myths.
They, too, run the unavoidable risk of becoming idols,
divine objects, instead of humanly constructed symbols
that may mediate, but can never enclose, the divine.

The important thing to remember here is that we cannot do without myths; they are the way we express and give form to our transcendent longing, our ultimate concern. But we must constantly reflect on the way they work and refuse to offer them any final status. This process is what theologians call 'demythologisation', which is a self-conscious act of reflection on how myths operate. To demythologise the myth of Adam and Eve, for instance, is not to abandon it as a uselessly primitive way of speaking about abstract matters. It is to understand it as a myth, a narrative way of speaking about abstractions, which is valued for that very reason. The myth is seen as a powerful metaphor and is kept because it provides us with a powerful shorthand for complex human experiences of alienation and regret. The question we ask of a myth, therefore, is not whether it is true or false, but whether it is living or dead. The main difference between a myth and one of Kuhn's scientific paradigms is that the equivalent in religion of a scientific revolution is not so much the discarding of myth as its re-interpretation, even the recognition, possibly for the first time, that it *is* myth, a narrative way of talking about complex human experiences.

Retaining, but demythologising a story in this way gives us what Tillich calls 'a broken myth'. He writes: 'A myth which is understood as a myth, but not removed or replaced, can be called "a broken myth". Christianity denies by its very nature any unbroken myth, because its presupposition is the first commandment: the affirmation of the ultimate as ultimate and the rejection of any kind of idolatry. All mythological elements in the Bible, and doctrine and liturgy should be recognised as mythological, but they should be maintained in their symbolic form and not be replaced by scientific substitutes. For there is no substitute for the use of symbols and myths: they are the language of faith.'[13] Tillich's account of the way we might re-interpret myth for our day is useful, but his language is unduly negative. The idea of 'a broken myth' suggests something that no longer works. A more useful way of describing the process would be to talk about 'breaking a myth open'. By opening it up we uncover its meaning for our own time. However, this process of breaking or re-interpreting the myth to release its power for our own day is always resisted by its official keepers. To challenge or criticise the myth of which they are the guardians not only threatens their authority, it threatens the peace and security of the people who have submitted themselves to the systems they control. This is why the people who challenge religion's claim to be a carrier of objective knowledge rather than the poet of symbol and metaphor are invariably denounced as faithless apostates. The irony here is that these prophetic challenges to the misuse of myth and symbol are usually made by people who have a radical fear of idolatry and who would rather fall into atheism than submit to the worship of human constructs, which is what the failure to recognise the real status of myth amounts to. Tillich is eloquent on the subject:

The resistance against demythologisation expresses itself in 'literalism.' The symbols and myths are understood in their immediate meaning. The material, taken from nature and history, is used in its proper sense. The character of the symbol to point beyond itself to something else is disregarded. Creation is taken as a magic act which happened once upon a time. The fall of Adam is localised on a special geographical point and attributed to a human individual. The virgin birth of the Messiah is understood in biological terms, resurrection and ascension as physical events, the second coming of Christ as a cosmic catastrophe. The presupposition of such literalism is that God is a being, acting in time and space, dwelling in a special place, affecting the course of events and being affected by them like any other being in the universe. Literalism deprives God of his ultimacy and, religiously speaking, of his majesty. It draws him down to the level of that which is not ultimate, the finite and conditional.[14]

He goes on to describe two stages of literalism, which he calls the 'natural' and the 'reactive'. In the natural stage of literalism the mythical and the literal are indistinguishable. This stage is characteristic of primitive individuals and groups who do not separate the creations of the imagination from natural facts. Tillich says that this stage has its own rights and should be left undisturbed right up to the time when humanity's questioning mind challenges the conventional acceptance of the myth as literal. There are only two ways to go when this moment arrives. The first is to replace the unbroken myth with the myth that has been broken open, and which now yields its inner meaning through interpretation and the power of metaphor. Unfortunately, many people find it impossible to live with a myth that has been broken open, so they repress their own questions and denounce the questions that others put to it. They retreat into reactive literalism, which is aware of the questions but represses them, either consciously or unconsciously. The instrument of repression is usually an acknowledged authority, which claims our unconditional surrender to its method of interpretation.

Natural literalism is obviously an honest response to myth and symbol. In Kuhnian language, it is to remain within an early paradigm that is working and still offers the best way of dealing with ongoing questions. Reactive literalism, on the other hand, is usually a rear-guard action on the part of those who are still emotionally invested in a fading paradigm. Their fear is that if the myth is understood in a different way it will lose its power. In the language of Anthony Giddens in *Beyond Left and Right*, they defend the tradition in the traditional way and thereby put it at risk. If religious narratives are to retain their power they must be capable of constant re-interpretation, must adapt to changing understandings of meaning. If this is made impossible, because of the anxieties of the guardians of the myth, then they will suffer the same fate as Aristotle's physics and Ptolemy's astronomy and they will be superseded. The fascinating thing here is that the conservative guardians of religion seem to misunderstand the nature of religion itself and thereby place it in great peril. They scientise religion and claim that it is about hard information, facts that must be accepted as 'true' rather than as mythic and symbolic ways of talking about the meaning and the mystery of life. If they succeed in their rear-guard campaign, Christianity will end up as a marginal sect. That may be its fate anyway, but it is too precious not to be fought for. Fortunately, there are countless numbers in the church who want to turn from this obsessive resistance to change and enlist Christianity in the great human adventure of mending the world and challenging human cruelty. It's a battle worth fighting.

PART TWO

Rebuilding the Ruins

They shall rebuild the ruined cities and inhabit
   them;
they shall plant vineyards and drink their wine,
and they shall make gardens and eat their fruit.

Amos 9.14

CHAPTER FIVE

Go Down Moses

So far in this book I have tried to adopt a certain tone of voice towards religion. Religion is an infinitely varied thing and it is always tempting to dismiss what others have made of it. Sometimes it is right to make these critical judgements, particularly if we recognise that there is a systemic contradiction between the claim and the life of those making the claim. Of what good is it to claim to know that God is all-merciful, if we ourselves do not try to practise mercy? Sometimes we have to challenge a particular school of interpretation because it is intrinsically cruel and abusive. The reason why many Christians are strongly opposed to literalist approaches to scripture is not because they think they are intellectually confused, but because they have a damaging impact upon certain groups of people, such as homosexuals. This was made brutally clear at the Lambeth Conference in 1998. At this meeting of Anglican bishops from round the world the most contentious issue before us concerned what the Bible says about homosexuality and whether it could be re-interpreted in the light of modern knowledge. 'No way', most of bishops declared, 'you cannot pick and mix with holy scripture. You take it or you leave it.' That is the kind of clarity the newspapers like and understand; and it gave them a wonderful news story. The trouble is, as with most black-or-white issues, the truth is more complicated than the headlines suggested. There is a letter on the internet originating from the United States that captures the complexity of it all. It purports to be written by a troubled Christian to Dr Laura, a fundamentalist agony aunt.

Dear Dr Laura,

Thank you for doing so much to educate people regarding God's Law. I have learned a great deal from you, and I try to share that knowledge with as many people as I can. When someone tries to defend the homosexual lifestyle, for example, I simply remind him that Leviticus 18.22 clearly states it to be an abomination. End of debate. I do need some advice from you, however, regarding one or two specific laws and how best to follow them.

a. When I burn a bull on the altar as a sacrifice, I know it creates a pleasing odour for the Lord (Lev.1.9). The problem is my neighbours. They claim the odour is not pleasing to them. How should I deal with this?

b. I would like to sell my daughter into slavery, as it suggests in Exodus 21.7. In this day and age, what do you think would be a fair price?

c. I know that I am allowed no contact with a woman while she is in her period of menstrual uncleanliness (Lev.15.19-24). The problem is, how do I tell? I have tried asking, but most women take offence.

d. Leviticus 25.44 states that I may buy slaves from the nations that are around us. A friend of mine claims that this applies to Mexicans, but not Canadians. Can you clarify?

e. I have a neighbour who insists on working on the Sabbath. Exodus 35.2 clearly states he should be put to death. Am I morally obligated to kill him myself?

f. A friend of mine feels that even though eating shellfish is an abomination (Lev.10.10), it is a lesser abomination than homosexuality. I don't agree. Can you settle this?

g. Leviticus 20.20 states that I may not approach the

altar of God if I have a defect in my sight. I have to admit that I wear reading glasses. Does my vision have to be 20/20, or is there some wiggle room here?

I know you have studied these things extensively, so I am confident you can help. Thank you for reminding us again that God's word is eternal and unchanging.

To use the Bible like an infallible law book that needs no interpretation is an absurd position to hold, but it only really matters when it prompts people to persecute their neighbours, as has been the case with the Church's treatment of homosexuals. However, in most circumstances it is usually better to leave people to the devices they have created to get themselves through life. Frank Sinatra said that he believed in anything that got him through the night. On a more profound level, I am haunted by some words in the greatest of the Holocaust novels, *The Last of the Just* by André Schwarz-Bart. The book is the story of Ernie Levy, the last of 'the just men', who died at Auschwitz in 1943. At the end of the story, Ernie is in a box car with some women and children, many of them already dead, lurching towards the death camp. It is Ernie's burden to console the inconsolable. The children gather round him for comfort as he cradles in his arms the emaciated corpse of a child who has just died of dysentery.

'He was my brother,' a little girl said hesitantly, anxiously, as though she had not decided what attitude it would be best to take in front of Ernie.

He sat down next to her and set her on his knees. 'He'll wake up too, in a little while, with all the others, when we reach the Kingdom of Israel. There children find their parents, and everybody is happy.

'Because the country we're going to, that's our kingdom, you know. There, the sun never sets, and you may eat anything you can think of. There, an eternal joy will crown your heads; cheerfulness and gaiety will come and greet you, and all the pains and all the moans will run away . . .'

'How can you tell them it's only a dream?' one of the women breathed, with hate in her voice. Rocking the child mechanically, Ernie gave way to dry sobs.

'Madame', he said at last, 'there is no room for truth here'. Then he stopped rocking the child, turned, and saw that the old woman's face had altered.

'Then what is there room for?' she began. And taking a closer look at Ernie, registering all the slightest details of his face, she murmured softly, 'Then you don't believe what you're saying at all? Not at all?'[1]

This book is unlikely to be read by those who are able to take the ancient narratives of religion at their face value as factual accounts of wonders performed by God long ago, and I have little desire to disturb their peace. 'Tread softly, for you tread on my dreams'[2] is not a bad motto for religious investigators. There are times when we should leave undisturbed what we may believe to be consoling fictions, and let people find what comfort they can against the emptiness or horror that confronts them. However, there are many others for whom none of the traditional approaches to the interpretation of scripture is honestly possible. It is for them that I write. I am trying to provide a way in which the great symbols and narratives of religion can be understood as human creations that express the depths and struggles of our own nature. In this chapter I want to apply that approach not to the Christian scriptures, but to the great narratives of the Hebrew Bible to see what use we can make of them. If you already have a love-enlarging way of using these narratives, you will not find the approach I am suggesting anything more than an intellectual curiosity. On the other hand, if you are intrigued by the great religious narratives, but have not found a way of adapting them to a life that seems to be cultures and aeons away from their world-view, maybe something useful will emerge in this approach. Something A.N. Wilson wrote in his book on St Paul will provide us with a useful point of entry. It is a little polemical, this quotation, and it reminds us that finding a form of religious discourse that fits us may sound like too peremptory a dismissal of approaches that work for others. Anyway, here is the quotation:

> The modern Christian 'fundamentalist' who bravely con-
> tinues to 'believe' in a real star of Bethlehem or an actual
> Garden Tomb in Jerusalem from which Jesus rose from
> the dead is making the same unimaginative mistake as
> Heinrich Schliemann when he dug in the sands of Hissarlik
> and thought he was finding Homer's Troy. Troy is in the
> Iliad, not in the sand. And because of Homer, not because
> of the sand, Troy exists in the collective consciousness of
> the human race.[3]

There is a whole world of significance in that idea of the collective consciousness of the human race, and it has particular importance when we meditate on the enduring power of the great religious narratives. They are archetypes that connect with the general condition of humanity; they speak of sorrow and loss, heroism and betrayal, faith and hope. This is why they go on touching us long after we have abandoned the official theories or teachings that have been derived from them. I would like to sketch a way in which we might use some of the great themes in the Hebrew scriptures for personal and social exploration, leading to human wholeness. The foundational event in the religion of the Hebrews, celebrated each year in the feast of the Passover, was the Exodus of the Israelites from Egypt, followed by forty years in the wilderness before their arrival in the promised land. There are several psalms, composed for use at major festivals, which recite this history, such as Psalm 106:

> [7] Our ancestors, when they were in Egypt,
>   did not consider your wonderful works;
> they did not remember the abundance of your
>   steadfast love,
>   but rebelled against the Most High at the Red Sea.
> [8] Yet he saved them for his name's sake,
>   so that he might make known his mighty power.
> [9] He rebuked the Red Sea, and it became dry;
>   he led them through the deep as through a desert.
> [10] So he saved them from the hand of the foe,
>   and delivered them from the hand of the enemy.
> [11] The waters covered their adversaries;
>   not one of them was left.
> [12] Then they believed his words;
>   they sang his praise.
>
> [13] But they soon forgot his works;
>   they did not wait for his counsel.
> [14] But they had a wanton craving in the wilderness,
>   and put God to the test in the desert;
>
> [19] They made a calf at Horeb
>   and worshiped a cast image.
> [20] They exchanged the glory of God
>   for the image of an ox that eats grass.
> [21] They forgot God, their Savior,
>   who had done great things in Egypt,
> [22] wondrous works in the land of Ham,
>   and awesome deeds by the Red Sea.

[24] Then they despised the pleasant land,
  having no faith in his promise.
[25] They grumbled in their tents,
  and did not obey the voice of the Lord.

[32] They angered the Lord at the waters of Meribah,
  and it went ill with Moses on their account;
[33] for they made his spirit bitter,
  and he spoke words that were rash.

[40] Then the anger of the Lord was kindled against
    his people,
  and he abhorred his heritage;
[41] he gave them into the hand of the nations,
  so that those who hated them ruled over them.
[42] Their enemies oppressed them,
  and they were brought into subjection under their
    power.
[43] Many times he delivered them,
  but they were rebellious in their purposes,
  and were brought low through their iniquity.
[44] Nevertheless he regarded their distress
  when he heard their cry.
[45] For their sake he remembered his covenant,
  and showed compassion according to the abundance of
    his steadfast love.
[46] He caused them to be pitied
  by all who held them captive.

[47] Save us, O Lord our God,
  and gather us from among the nations,
that we may give thanks to your holy name
  and glory in your praise.

Whatever the nature of these ancient events, the story
of the children of Israel can clearly be used as a way

of interpreting the human experience. There are three complex and enduring human experiences expressed by the ancient biblical narratives. There is the theme of Falling into Captivity; there is the theme of Liberation through the Wilderness; finally, there is the Discovery of the Promised Land and the Regret and Disillusion that accompany it. The complement to the theme of Fall in the Hebrew Scriptures is the theme of Captivity or bondage in Egypt. I am not suggesting that the texts leap from Fall to Captivity to disillusion, but there is a sort of narrative logic to the scheme that reflects human experience. Our discontents lead us into experiences that begin by exhilarating us, gradually turn into habits that bore us, and can end by trapping us in relationships or routines that imprison us. And there is nothing that cannot be the vehicle of this process: natural substances, sex, emotional entanglements, greed for status and the toys it buys, work, spirituality, religion. Any of these, or any combination of these, can be the force that arrests and imprisons us. Breaking out and making it to freedom is tough.

There are not too many human themes or archetypes, but falling into discontent and then falling through discontent into some sort of prison or captivity is clearly one of them. We can see it at its most dramatic in the simplest and starkest of the human dramas, that of addiction bred of deprivation. If you are a young man living without hope in a desperate housing scheme in New York or Glasgow, then heroin is going to offer you a way out of your discontent, for a time and at a price. It's the Sinatra imperative again, something to get you through the long night of the soul, to dull the pain, to lead you into merciful oblivion. There may be ways of escape, mechanisms of fall, that do not have terrible landings, but they do not seem to have been invented yet. The cruellest part of the human paradox of discontent is that the instrument of escape all too easily becomes the place of imprisonment. The substance that takes us out of ourselves, or the secret relationship that gives us something to live for, can become the instrument that takes away our peace.

In the case of the addict, no matter the nature of the dependence, the means of release inevitably become the bondage from which there is no escape. Addiction seems to be one of the characteristics of our era. It may have something to do with the apparently limitless productiveness of global capitalism that has to go on generating new needs all the time, because the one thing it cannot do is stand still. G.K. Galbraith has described the affluent classes in our era as inhabiting a culture of contentment that insulates them from the misery of the poor, and that is undoubtedly a valid way to describe our society. But there is also a lot of evidence of emotional or spiritual discontent among the prosperous, especially in the area of human relationships. We seem less content to play the hand that life has dealt us than our forebears were, and the price we pay is a drifting search for an elusive contentment, because there is always the promise of something more complete, something or someone more comprehensively satisfying. I am desperate to avoid a tone of condemnation here, mainly because I do not believe people are entirely responsible for the choices they make, but there is as much to regret as to celebrate in the human situation of our time. There is something poignant about our longing for perfect lives, and something in me admires people for refusing to settle for less than what they deem to be the best. The wisdom of the ancient narratives would suggest that the first place to look for a reason for our unhappiness is to our own failings. Scripture can be used as an instrument of Socratic interrogation. If we use it to question the nature of our own discontents, it will help us to identify the mechanisms of blame we have constructed to shield ourselves from our own responsibility for the way things are with us.

So far I have implied that these dramas of Fall and Captivity happen to individuals, and it is certainly true that most of my emphasis will be on the personal use of the great narratives in the struggles of our private lives, but a more profound example of this theme is provided by whole communities. Whole peoples and races can be led into captivity by the compulsions of oppressing power, and the same psychological mechanisms apply, the same dynamic of final self-imprisonment. Any community that creates slaves or serfs ends up imprisoned by the very system that is meant to amplify its freedom. So it is no surprise that the most dramatic and effective use of the great biblical narratives of captivity and the struggle to be free has been made by enslaved peoples, by Afro-Americans, by the oppressed people in South and Central America and Africa, by those anywhere who have found themselves in bondage and heard the great story of Israel's escape from Egypt into the wilderness and the long trek to the promised land. This rhetoric of exodus and wilderness marks the speeches of Martin Luther King and the Black Theology movement in North America. It also marks the Liberation Theology of Central and South America. I visited a Base Community in El Salvador during the civil war in 1990, weeks after a massacre of Jesuit priests at the university, and heard an exposition of scripture that burned with passion from a man who lived in a plywood shack in a shanty town. He was interpreting the passage in Luke where Jesus reads from a verse in Isaiah that proclaims good news to the poor, release for prisoners, recovery of sight for the blind, and letting broken victims go free. This was no application from a distance, no spiritualising of the text to make it fit a very different context: the fit was perfect, it was about their situation, it described their experience, it was about their struggle for liberation; it was living scripture, their scripture, their narrative. This active, political use of the narratives is still powerfully appropriate and it is why oppressed groups anywhere are easily able to find themselves in these ancient texts and use them in a living way. In addition to providing oppressed groups with theological ammunition and stunning metaphors, they have also produced some great songs, none better than the spirituals sung by the slaves in the United States during their long trek to freedom.

> Go down, Moses,
> 'Way down in Egypt land,
> Tell ole Pharoah,
> To let my people go.[4]

But let me return to the less exciting theme of personal captivity and the struggle for wholeness and freedom that is likely to be the most immediate use we shall make of these texts. The narratives are remorseless in their announcement to us that there are no easy routes to personal wholeness and human freedom. The long process of liberation may begin in exciting euphoria, in a midnight flight from Egypt, in an act of stunning resolution, but it is always followed by the long trek through the wilderness. This long trudge of discipline is true in all our human predicaments, but it is agonisingly true of the compulsions that afflict us and from which we long to grow and move away.

There may be support systems, maintenance programmes, therapy and counselling, prayer and re-assurance, but there is no shortcut through the dry lands of effort. Growth is a cumulative process. Of course, it will not start at all without the strength that comes from the longing for freedom and the loving challenge our friends place before us, but once we are on the road we have to walk it. As far as our compulsions are concerned, it is a bit like slowly rewinding the tape of our days. The habits that imprison us were gradually wound round our lives by the slow accumulations of imprisoning habit, and they can only be unwound by the same process, slowly reversed. No violence or suddenness will work; the human psyche is not equipped with a fast rewind button; but tips and techniques can help us along bits of the way. Nietzsche thought a lot about this. He said that there were only six ways of combating the vehemence of a drive. First, there is the avoidance of the opportunities for gratification of the drive, so that it will become progressively weakened till it withers away. Or we can impose a pattern of strict regularity in the gratification of the drive, so that we gain intervals of peace during which we are not troubled, and maybe go on from there to the first method. Thirdly, we can deliberately give ourselves over to the wild and unrestrained gratification of the drive in order to generate disgust with it and use the disgust to get power over the drive. There is what he calls the intellectual artifice of associating gratification of the drive with painful thoughts, so that the gratification itself becomes painful. Number five tells us to bring about a dislocation of the amount of strength we have by taking up particularly difficult and strenuous labours, or by deliberately subjecting ourselves to a new stimulus and pleasure that redirects our thoughts and urges it into other channels. In this regard, Bishop Gore spoke of 'the expulsive power of a new affection', and certainly nothing is better at casting out the bitterness and sorrow of an old love affair than entering into a new one. Finally, and rather despairingly, Nietzsche suggests that, for those of us who can endure it, we should weaken and depress our whole bodily organisation by ascetical practices, so that in the overall weakening that occurs the particular drive that is disturbing us will be weakened as well.[5] Nietzsche was a profound psychologist and I have quoted that guidance because it shows what tough territory we are in when we start working on ourselves. The forty years wandering in the wilderness, with all its temptations and complaints, is an apt symbol of the human struggle for peace and wholeness. And no one gets it easy, or no one of any complexity.

What happens when we finally make it to the promised land of sobriety or relational stability or the mastery of some discipline or career? From a distance, the promised estate flowed with milk and honey and, from the heat and deprivation of the desert, that looked exactly like what we wanted. But who could or would want to live on milk and honey for the rest of their lives? It might be a good way to start the day, but as an invariable diet? Let's face it, it cloys, it soon has us longing for something more exciting, even for the diet of the wilderness, the manna and the quails, those moments of self-mastery and the mysterious contentment that the struggle itself brought us. What happens in the promised land is exactly what started the whole thing going in the first place, in the place called Egypt that held us captive. What gets going again is what never really stopped, though it was perhaps too exhausted or depressed to be really obnoxious for a while, and that is *ourself*. *We* come into the promised land along with all our ideals and longings, and pretty soon we are up to our old tricks. When I was in South Africa on the day the Truth Commission produced its report, I witnessed this depressingly ancient human reality. Of all the groups in South Africa that took part in the long struggle in the wilderness years of apartheid, who would have expected the ANC to try to block the publication of the report of those terrible years? But they did, along with Mr de Klerk, because a number of the Commission's findings reflected harshly on aspects of their role during the long years of struggle. And Desmond Tutu, that true prophet, true in the wilderness, still true in the promised land, pointed out that he had not struggled to liberate slaves in order for them to become oppressors. That is always the struggle, the eternal struggle of the human heart. It is what turns God's ancient persecuted people, the Jews, into the persecutors of the Palestinians in their own land. It is what makes the man who, in the parable of Jesus, is forgiven a mountain of debt into the persecutor of the poor man who owed him a handful. It is the failure to connect, the failure of identification, the failure of the imagination of the heart. That is why the struggle is never over, the promised land never finally delivers the promise, unless we remember the most important of the lessons that good religion teaches us: we ourselves are never cured of ourselves; we are always, in New Testament language, sinners in need of forgiveness and grace. Unfortunately, Christianity has turned that healthy realism about human nature into something rather diseased and dangerous in its claim that we are all born guilty of original sin.

CHAPTER SIX

Blaming Eve

One Sunday night when I was a young priest I came home from evensong, had my supper and was reading the newspaper when the phone rang. It was a ward sister at a local hospital, asking if I would go to the hospital immediately, because parishioners of mine were in need of pastoral ministration. I hastened over to the hospital and found a man I knew slightly who informed me that his wife had just given birth to premature triplets who were not expected to live out the night and would I please baptise them. This kind of ceremony is called emergency baptism and I agreed to do it immediately. I was taken to the room where the three tiny scraps of life were lying in incubators and I asked for a cup of water. Then I reached into the containers where the three babies lay and marked each one's head with water and baptised all three of them 'In the name of the Father and of the Son and of the Holy Spirit', according to the ancient formula. They all died a few hours later.

What I had done was an act of pastoral care for the parents of the tiny babies and it did, indeed, provide them with a certain bleak comfort. I had responded to the request of the parents out of care for them, but behind the practice of emergency baptism there lies one of the most unsympathetic of the Christian doctrines. It is the doctrine that the unbaptised go to hell after death, hence the need to administer baptism without preparation in situations of imminent death. The doctrine was later slightly modified in the case of babies who, though they were born guilty of original sin like everyone else, had not had time to commit any actual sins, so they had their sentences commuted to eternity in the *limbo puerorum*, or suburb of children, from the Latin *limbus* for edge or border. Voltaire claimed that limbo was invented by Peter Chrysologos in the fifth century as a sort of mitigated hell for babies who died before baptism, 'and where resided the patriarchs before the descent of Jesus Christ into hell; so that the view that Jesus Christ descended to limbo and not into hell has prevailed since then'.[1] Thinking about the fate of unbaptised babies is the cleanest way to tackle the keystone doctrine of the whole Christian theological system, the doctrine of original sin, because it saves us from getting mixed up with the doctrine of punishment for sins committed rather than inherited, actual sin as contrasted with original sin.

There is a certain moral logic in the notion of punishment after death for sins actually committed in life, and most of the great religions have versions of it. Buddhism and Hinduism see it more as a process of impersonal consequences rather than as the personally imposed punishment by God we find in the Christian tradition, but there is a certain logic in either approach: what you sow you reap, acts have consequences. In the doctrine of punishment by God after death there may be more than a trace of the resentment that Nietzsche despised in the Christian tradition, the hatred that the weak have for the strong and their longing to get their revenge upon them, even if they had to wait for the afterlife in which to do so. There may also be an instinctive sense of justice of the sort expressed in the parable of Dives and Lazarus. In that parable, versions of which are found in various religious traditions, the rich man implores Abraham for a little comfort and is refused it because he has already used up his comfort account: 'He called out, "Father Abraham, have mercy on me, and send Lazarus to dip the tip of his finger in water and cool my tongue; for I am in agony in these flames." But Abraham said, "Child, remember that during your lifetime you received your good things, and Lazarus in like manner evil things; but now he is comforted here, and you are in agony." '[2] Even if we do not believe in the morality of eternal punishment for temporal crimes, we can follow the reasoning that leads to the concept of the afterlife as a place where the inequalities of this life are evened out and balanced up. Many of our most ancient stories are based on this deep longing for justice, for wrongs to be righted and villains to be punished, and since it does not seem to happen in this life in any balanced or systematic way, it is easy to understand how the human imagination projected the final reckoning on to the afterlife. Whatever we make of this kind of thing ourselves, it is easy to understand its moral logic and even to admire its effectiveness as a deterrent to wickedness.

The Christian doctrine of original sin and its remedy lacks this kind of moral dimension. It reduces the matter either to the application of a ceremony that wipes out the balance sheet of sin, whether original or actual, by virtue of its enactment; or to the acceptance by the believer of a particular form of words concerning Jesus that has the same effect. This was one reason why baptism was abused in the early Church among those who wanted the best of both worlds, this one and the next. Voltaire gives a mordant example of the abuse: 'This sacrament was abused in the first centuries of Christianity; nothing was so common as to await the final agony in order to receive baptism. The example of the emperor Constantine is pretty good proof of that. This is how he reasoned: baptism purifies everything; I can therefore kill my wife, my son and all my relations; after which I shall have myself baptised and I shall go to heaven; and in fact that is just what he did.'[3]

The specifically Christian element in the ancient drama of human folly and frailty, therefore, seems to have two ethically dubious elements, one of which is the doctrine of original sin itself and the other the claim that, by the application of a particular ceremony or the holding of a particular belief in the head, the debt inherited by the human plaintiff can be converted to credit in the divine balance sheet. Both of these elements essentially reduce the resolution of the human drama to a mental act, the holding of a particular opinion, followed by a ceremonial action that is automatically, if mystically, efficacious. This is not a phenomenon that is confined to Christianity, but there it has created a specific kind of mentalism called dogmatism, which is the belief that holding right ideas in our head can save us from damnation, just as holding wrong ones can condemn us to it. How did it all come about?

Well, we cannot blame the story of the tempting of Adam and Eve in the Hebrew scriptures because the doctrine of original sin and consequent congenital guilt is not found there, as we will discover when we read chapter 3 of Genesis:

[3:1] Now the serpent was more crafty than any other wild animal that the Lord God had made. He said to the woman, 'Did God say, "You shall not eat from any tree in the garden"?' [2] The woman said to the serpent, 'We may eat of the fruit of the trees in the garden; [3] but God said, "You shall not eat of the fruit of the tree that is in the middle of the garden, nor shall you touch it, or you shall die."' [4] But the serpent said to the woman, 'You will not die; [5] for God knows that when you eat of it your eyes will be opened, and you will be like God, knowing good and evil.' [6] So when the woman saw that the tree was good for food, and that it was a delight to the eyes, and that the tree was to be desired to make one wise, she took of its fruit and ate; and she also gave some to her husband, who was with her, and he ate. [7] Then the eyes of both were opened, and they knew that they were naked; and they sewed fig leaves together and made loincloths for themselves.

[8] They heard the sound of the Lord God walking in the garden at the time of the evening breeze, and the man and his wife hid themselves from the presence of the Lord God among the trees of the garden. [9] But the Lord God called to the man, and said to him, 'Where are you?' [10] He said, 'I heard the sound of you in the garden, and I was afraid, because I was naked; and I hid myself.' [11] He said, 'Who told you that you were naked? Have you eaten from the tree of which I commanded you not to eat?' [12] The man said, 'The woman whom you gave to be with me, she gave me fruit from the tree, and I ate.' [13] Then the Lord God said to the woman, 'What is this that you have done?' The woman said, 'The serpent tricked me, and I ate.' [14] The Lord God said to the serpent,

'Because you have done this,
    cursed are you among all animals
    and among all wild creatures;
upon your belly you shall go,
    and dust you shall eat
    all the days of your life.
[15] I will put enmity between you and the woman,

and between your offspring and hers;
he will strike your head,
and you will strike his heel.'
[16] To the woman he said,
'I will greatly increase your pangs in childbearing;
in pain you shall bring forth children,
yet your desire shall be for your husband,
and he shall rule over you.'
[17] And to the man he said,
'Because you have listened to the voice of your
wife,
and have eaten of the tree
about which I commanded you,
"You shall not eat of it,"
cursed is the ground because of you;
in toil you shall eat of it all the days of your life;
[18] thorns and thistles it shall bring forth for you;
and you shall eat the plants of the field.
[19] By the sweat of your face
you shall eat bread
until you return to the ground,
for out of it you were taken;
you are dust,
and to dust you shall return.'

Whatever we make of this ancient narrative, it says nothing about the transmission of Adam's guilt to humanity and it is interpreted by Jewish scholars as an allegory of the human condition, not necessarily as a historic event. It is a myth, not a factual account of a real event. St Paul seems to have been the first person in the Christian tradition to treat it as a historic event from which conclusions could be drawn and consequences measured. Paul's account comes in his Letter to the Romans, chapter 5:

[12] Therefore, just as sin came into the world through one

man, and death came through sin, and so death spread to
all because all have sinned –

[17] If, because of the one man's trespass, death exercised dominion through that one, much more surely will
those who receive the abundance of grace and the free gift
of righteousness exercise dominion in life through the one
man, Jesus Christ.

[18] Therefore just as one man's trespass led to condemnation for all, so one man's act of righteousness leads
to justification and life for all. [19] For just as by the
one man's disobedience the many were made sinners,
so by the one man's obedience the many will be made
righteous.

In this passage Paul emphasises that death was the punishment for Adam's sin, the implication being that if Adam
had not sinned he would not have died. It is possible, of
course, to read the idea of original sin and inherited guilt
into Paul's words, but it is not as clearly stated there
as it was later by Augustine of Hippo, who is usually
credited with the invention of the fully developed idea.
However, Peter Brown, the greatest modern interpreter
of Augustine, has pointed out that 'The idea that some
ancient sin lay behind the misery of the human condition
was shared by pagans and Christians in Late Antiquity.'
He tells us that Augustine had met the idea in his early
life as a Catholic and he goes on to quote him and to add
his own comment:

'The Ancient Sin: nothing is more obviously part of our
preaching of Christianity; yet nothing is more impene-
trable to the understanding' ... while many Catholics
in Africa and Italy already believed that the 'first sin' of
Adam had somehow been inherited by his descendants,
Augustine will tell them precisely where they should look

in themselves for abiding traces of this first sin. With the fatal ease of a man who believes that he can explain a complex phenomenon, simply by reducing it to its historical origins, Augustine will remind his congregation of the exact circumstances of the Fall of Adam and Eve. When they had disobeyed God by eating the forbidden fruit, they had been 'ashamed': they had covered their genitals with fig leaves. That was enough for Augustine: 'Ecce unde'. 'That's the place! That's the place from which the first sin is passed on.' This shame at the uncontrollable stirring of the genitals was the fitting punishment of the crime of disobedience. Nothing if not circumstantial, Augustine will drive his point home by suddenly appealing to his congregation's sense of shame at night emissions . . . Thus at one stroke, Augustine will draw the boundary between the positive and negative elements in human nature along a line dividing the conscious, rational mind from the one 'great force' that escaped its control.[4]

If we refuse to treat ancient myths as the record of historical events, we can use our imagination to guess how they came to develop. The main elements in the story of the Fall are clearly death, toil and shame, and the myth clearly offers an explanatory narrative for these overpowering human experiences. Augustine's isolation of sexual shame as the main element in the Fall story is interestingly echoed in one of Freud's most brilliant guesses, where he wonders whether shame and sexual embarrassment entered the human psyche when *homo sapiens* assumed vertical posture and exposed its genitalia.[5] Another mythical guess about the pains and fascinations of human sexuality is found in Plato's *Symposium*, in Aristophanes' famous myth:

The starting point is for you to understand human nature

and what has happened to it. You see, our nature wasn't originally the same as it is now: it has changed. Firstly, there used to be three human genders, not just two – male and female – as there are nowadays. There was also a third, which was a combination of both the other two. Its name has survived, but the gender itself has died out. In those days there was a distinct type of androgynous person, not just the word, though like the word the gender combined male and female; nowadays, however, only the word remains, and that counts as an insult.[6]

Aristophanes' myth is a long one, but it is clearly intended to explain the varieties of sexual longing. The key element in the myth is the decision by Zeus and the other gods to divide human creatures into two halves, because of their dangerous challenge to divine power. Thereafter they will have to spend much of their energy trying to complete themselves by finding and joining up with their other half. Here's how he sees it working out.

Any men who are offcuts from the combined gender – the androgynous one – are attracted to women, and therefore most adulterers come from this group; the equivalent women are attracted to men and tend to become adulteresses. Any women who are offcuts from the female gender aren't particularly interested in men; they incline more towards women, and therefore female homosexuality comes from this group. And any men who are offcuts from the male gender go for males.[7]

It is interesting to speculate about what might have become of the Christian attitude to sexuality if the Church had borrowed its myths from Greek rather than Hebrew tradition, as it did in the third and fourth century with many of its philosophical and theological ideas. Had that happened,

Christian fundamentalists today might be pointing to the inerrant book of Aristophanes to explain their passionate support for gay and lesbian rights which were being threatened by revisionist liberals who refused to accept the historical validity of the speeches in the *Symposium*.

Apart from trying to offer an explanation for the great human themes of sexuality and death, the ancient myths of humanity try to account for human misery by narratives of catastrophe and Fall from an original Eden. This is still a powerful theme, even today, and books are occasionally produced by nostalgic writers describing how wonderful Britain or, more usually, England was in the past before it was overrun by foreigners and contemporary corruption. Most of us are prone to this kind of thing from time to time, and some people seem to be chronically addicted to it. They hate the present time and look back fondly to some imagined perfection or golden age in the past. Some of this is ordinary mourning for our own lost youth, and Housman was probably its most bitter-sweet laureate:

> Into my heart an air that kills
>   From yon far country blows:
> What are those blue remembered hills,
>   What spires, what farms are those?
>
> That is the land of lost content,
>   I see it shining plain,
> The happy highways where I went
>   And cannot come again.[8]

As the blind poet Borges reminded us, all our paradises are lost paradises, places of contentment we destroyed by our own folly and greed. All of this is true enough, and we go on doing it to ourselves. Narratives of the

Fall or dystopias are probably more frequent in human history than narratives of paradise or utopias, because we seem to have a greater capacity for destroying than for creating contentment. The latest Fall narrative is global warming and consumer greed. Our own insatiable desires have the pyrrhic effect of fouling our own nest. It is the oldest story in the book, because it is the most constant of the human experiences. And it is even possible to find contemporary resonances in the notion of original sin or of inheriting some kind of taint. We are all familiar with the important emphasis that is now laid upon our earliest and most formative years. Psychologists have familiarised us with the kind of childhood traumas that some people never recover from and that mark most of us in some way or other. None of us chooses our parents, nor did they choose theirs, so each generation is given a hand to play that they did not ask for, sometimes with tragic consequences.

The difference in our myth of fall and loss today is that it comes mainly from science, which is the great narrative of our time. The language of Fall has been replaced by the language of struggle and ascent, and we are all familiar with drawings of the gradual emergence of *homo sapiens* from previous versions of the human species, right back to the primates who were our original ancestors. In today's creation myth, there never was an Eden, a perfect and innocent human state, with fully formed humans who knew no sin. Our narrative today is just as epic and exciting, but it is a sort of reverse catastrophe, as it traces the emergence of consciousness from a violent and exploding universe. One way of describing the human epic could go like this. There is a well-known aphorism: 'To know all is to forgive all.' The idea behind the saying is that

humans are largely determined by circumstances beyond
their control and that if we could see all the factors that
have led to a particular event in a person's life we would
fully understand and fully forgive. The philosophical term
for this point of view is 'determinism'. It holds that we
are not really the freely determined creatures we think
we are. We are, in fact, programmed by factors that are
beyond our control. Most of us would agree with this
point of view to some extent. We would acknowledge, for
instance, that if you are a young man reared by a single
mother living in poverty in a deprived housing estate you
are more likely to get a lousy education, more likely to get
in trouble with the law, more likely to be unemployed,
more likely to have bad health and more likely to die
young than if you were born to middle-class parents who
sent you to a private school. We may not be full-blooded
philosophical determinists, but experience teaches us that
external circumstances have a lot to do with how our life
works out. One of the oldest debates in politics is over
just how important external circumstances are in making
us what we are and what the role of private choice is.
The most interminable discussion in political theory is
whether systems make people or people make systems;
whether, in order to change people, you have to change
the system, or whether, in order to change the system,
you have to change people. All I want to register here
is the fact that human beings are made what they are by
millions of facts they are not in control of; and if we want
to understand ourselves we have to go deep and wide into
our past. To understand ourselves today, we have to have
some knowledge of where we have come from, and that
knowledge must apply to the emergence of our species as
well as the history of our own family.

We humans have only been around in the universe for a comparatively short period of time. According to the current narrative, the universe was born in violence, in what physicists call the Big Bang. Wherever it came from, it is a story of power exploding and expanding through space. Most of it seems to have been inert or lifeless till about three and a half billion years ago when the first self-replicating molecules came along and life began. On and on it goes, this amazing force of life. That's what makes nature programmes on TV so fascinating, as we look in on the great food chain that nature is, as we watch all the breeding and hunting and searching for food and building nests and stalking prey that is played out endlessly on our planet. Look out on any tranquil country scene on a summer's day and you might be deceived into illusions of peace and calm. In fact, underneath it all, life is killing and munching and swarming and breeding and dying. And it is that ability to look at what is happening, out there or inside ourselves, that is characteristic of our species, the human animal, or the *moral* animal, as the new science of evolutionary psychology defines us. In us the life-force has become conscious and we have started watching ourselves doing the things that come naturally or instinctively in the animal kingdom. Aspects of living that would pose little difficulty in a species that had not developed consciousness create major issues for us, as all the Fall myths amply indicate. Sex is still the obvious example, but our explanatory sexual narratives are different today. One school of evolutionary psychologists claims that the problem for the human male is that his DNA has programmed him to be a self-replicating animal, a seed-scattering machine without conscience; but this urge is in conflict with his consciousness, his self-awareness, because he is able to recognise that simply operating like a gene-propulsion machine can be damaging to others as well as to himself. Sex is not the only instinct that gets complicated by human development; violence and cruelty are also in there, programmed into us before the dawn of consciousness. So we are creatures who are in conflict with ourselves, *moral* animals, creatures in whom the life-force has started observing itself.

I have compressed millions of years of emergent consciousness into a few paragraphs there, but the point I am making is understandable enough. Human consciousness and the emergence of our moral sense move us away from the purely instinctive, the unconscious and unreflective natural response, to what we might call an *intentional* approach to life. The narrative of our day is not about having fallen from a perfect state, but about the endless search for a perfect state somewhere in the future. Our current myth is not about having fallen from a past perfection, but about the possibility of achieving a future perfection, and it characterises everything we do, from the search for the perfect kitchen to the quest for the perfect orgasm. That is why we encourage boys to sublimate their anger and aggression and be sensitive to the needs of others – whereas our instinctive hard-wiring accorded great survival value to the very impulses that have become so problematic for us in relationships today. Indeed, one major critical account of the undoubted male crisis of our time locates its cause right at this point, at what is called the feminisation of culture and the consequent discounting and disapproval of the purely masculine virtues of raw sexuality and aggression. I saw a little piece in the papers the other day about the male craze for body-building. The point that was being made was that it is difficult for men nowadays to know what the distinctive male role is, but they do know that they have a distinctive musculature, so they develop that to the point of exaggeration. They call this 'the Adonis complex', and there's more than a touch of it in the Kevin Spacey role in the Oscar winning film, *American Beauty* where, just as his life starts falling apart, he starts to build up his body.

Culture critics have a field day with this sort of stuff, but the point behind it all is that, as conscious animals, we are a problem to ourselves, as our myths, ancient and modern, amply illustrate. We will go on producing myths, ways of explaining ourselves to ourselves but, like everything else about us, they are in constant transition and we must not fundamentalise any of them. In spite of what the Christian doctrine of original sin claims, we are not guilty because we were born of parents who fell from perfection. Nevertheless, the myth is still eloquent and instructive not because it describes an ancient catastrophe, but because it expresses permanent human realities. Unfortunately, the fully developed Christian theological system treated the myth as historic fact from which human consequences could be deduced, such as the importance of baptising babies in danger of imminent death. And it brings us right up against the grimmest of the Christian doctrines, the belief in hell.

CHAPTER SEVEN

Heart of Darkness

On a Sunday morning one summer I went to church in Salisbury. The church, a beautifully light and airy building, was medieval, but the service was pleasantly modern, like thousands of others held at the same hour. The whole tone of the service, while not exactly stirring, was gently Anglican. There was no sense of captivating awe or overwhelming emotion of any sort; everything was decent and orderly, nothing to set the blood racing. And high above this quiet activity soared the chancel arch, and over the arch there was a medieval doom painting. While we exchanged the kiss of peace with good-natured self-consciousness, demons with long forked tails were thrusting tormented souls into hell. I returned to that painting repeatedly during the service, and the incongruity of it all struck me with considerable force. There was clearly little or no relationship between what was happening below and what was happening above. Once there would have been a solid connection between what was done or said in that church and the gruesome painting that dominated the entrance to the sanctuary.

The fires of hell are no longer regularly stoked in mainstream Christian pulpits, but the threat of hellfire used to be one of the most powerful and effective weapons in the Church's evangelistic armoury. Here is a fictional example of the kind of preaching that probably satisfied something of the human need to be scared witless that is now only catered for by the Hollywood horror film. It comes from James Joyce's, *Portrait of the Artist as a Young Man:*

> The torment of fire is the greatest torment to which the tyrant has ever subjected his fellow creatures. Place your finger for a moment in the flame of a candle and you will feel the pain of fire. But our earthly fire was created by God for the benefit of man, to maintain in him the spark of life and to help in the useful arts, whereas the fire of hell is of another quality and was created by God to torture and punish the unrepentant sinner. Our earthly fire also consumes more or less rapidly according as the object which it attacks is more or less combustible, so that human ingenuity has even succeeded in inventing chemical preparations to check or frustrate its action. But the sulphurous brimstone which burns in hell is a substance which is specially designed to burn for ever and for ever with unspeakable fury. Moreover, our earthly fire destroys at the same time as it burns, so that the more intense it is the shorter is its duration; but the fire of hell has this property, that it preserves that which it burns, and, though it rages with incredible intensity, it rages for ever.
>
> Our earthly fire again, no matter how fierce or wide-spread it may be, is always of a limited extent; but the lake of fire in hell is boundless, shoreless and bottomless. And this terrible fire will not afflict the bodies of the damned only from without, but each lost soul will be a hell unto itself, the boundless fire raging in its very vitals. O, how terrible is the lot of those wretched beings! The blood seethes and boils in the veins, the brains are boiling in the skull, the heart in the breast glowing and bursting, the bowels a red-hot mass of burning pulp, the tender eyes flaming like molten balls.[1]

You can imagine the effect of a sermon like that on a congregation of adolescent boys. It was meant to build an overwhelming fear into them, as the great preventive against sexual sin. An Oxford don was reported to have warned his audience of young men against the sins of the flesh by crying out, 'Why risk your eternal soul for the sake of a pleasure, which, I am reliably informed, lasts less than ninety seconds?' Even if you believe that masturbation is sinful, most people would agree that there is a gross disproportion here between the offence and the punishment. It seems fairly obvious that hell was meant to act as a preventive against sin, but there was another, even uglier, side to it than that. This was brought out by Nietzsche, in one of his withering asides on Christianity. Describing the Christian vision of heaven, he writes: 'For what is it that constitutes the bliss of this Paradise? We might even guess, but it is better to have it expressly described for us by an authority not to be underestimated in such matters, Thomas Aquinas, the great teacher and saint: "The blessed in the kingdom of heaven", he says, meek as a lamb, "will see the punishments of the damned, in order that their bliss be that much greater." '[2] So hell provides both punishment and pleasure. It is torment for the damned who endure it, but bliss for the redeemed in heaven who observe it. How can we account for the emergence and development of this, the most disturbing of the great Christian myths? Let me offer a few suggestions.

Originally *Sheol* or the place of the dead was thought of as a dark place of shadows beyond God's sight:

[3] For my soul is full of troubles,
    and my life draws near to Sheol.
[4] I am counted among those who go down to the Pit;
    I am like those who have no help,
[5] like those forsaken among the dead,
    like the slain that lie in the grave,

like those whom you remember no more,
for they are cut off from your hand.[3]

Gradually *Sheol* came to be thought of as a place of punishment. There is a body of writing in both the Hebrew and Christian scriptures called 'apocalyptic', from a Greek word meaning to reveal or uncover. Literature of this sort is mainly about the intervention of God to vindicate God's poor and righteous ones. Apocalyptic longing begins as the religion of oppressed people, and the psychology of its development is fairly obvious. If you are an impoverished peasant, taxed into destitution by the callous rulers whose greed starves your own children, a burning resentment against them is bound to rise within you, and a passionate longing for justice and vindication. You want to overturn the system that so cruelly oppresses you and your loved ones, but you want more than that. Justice demands that those who have trampled upon your humanity should be punished for what they have done to you. One of the marks of the great schemes of apocalyptic prediction is the condemnation and punishment of those who have exploited the poor in this life. There is a taunt over the king of Babylon in the Book of Isaiah that expresses this mood:

[14:1] But the Lord will have compassion on Jacob and will again choose Israel, and will set them in their own land; and aliens will join them and attach themselves to the house of Jacob. [2] And the nations will take them and bring them to their place, and the house of Israel will possess the nations as male and female slaves in the Lord's land; they will take captive those who were their captors, and rule over those who oppressed them.

[3] When the Lord has given you rest from your pain

and turmoil and the hard service with which you were made to serve, [4] you will take up this taunt against the king of Babylon:

How the oppressor has ceased!
 How his insolence has ceased!
[5] The Lord has broken the staff of the wicked,
 the scepter of rulers,
[6] that struck down the peoples in wrath
 with unceasing blows,
that ruled the nations in anger
 with unrelenting persecution.
[7] The whole earth is at rest and quiet;
 they break forth into singing.
[8] The cypresses exult over you,
 the cedars of Lebanon, saying,
'Since you were laid low,
 no one comes to cut us down.'
[9] Sheol beneath is stirred up
 to meet you when you come;
it rouses the shades to greet you,
 all who were leaders of the earth;
it raises from their thrones
 all who were kings of the nations.
[10] All of them will speak
 and say to you:
'You too have become as weak as we!
 You have become like us!'
[11] Your pomp is brought down to Sheol,
 and the sound of your harps;
maggots are the bed beneath you,
 and worms are your covering.[4]

There is a compelling moral logic in this, but it is intriguing that, in the West, it took the direction it did. In the East it went in a different direction. There the moral logic that

requires the satisfaction of justice went in the direction of
the doctrine of *karma*.

Two of the most important concepts in Hinduism are
samsara and *karma*. We are probably more familiar with
the terms *re-incarnation* or *transmigration of souls* than
with *samsara*. *Samsara*, which is found in Buddhism as
well as Hinduism, refers to the endless cycle of re-birth
that characterises the life of humanity. The soul of one
who dies does not pass into a permanent state of being,
such as heaven or hell; rather, it is reborn into another
existence, which itself will come to an end and lead to
another re-birth, and so on. The nature of the next re-birth
is determined by the law of *karma*, which means deeds or
works. How we live in this incarnation determines our
status in future births. What we sow we reap. The process
is impersonal; there is no judge or judgement, just the
endless repetitions of an ethically interconnected universe.
This approach seems to lack the voyeuristic ugliness of the
developed doctrine of hell in the West, though there may
well be a certain satisfaction to be had from knowing that
the overweening tyrant who is making life such a trial for
you may have the tables turned on him during his next
go-round. But something of the effect is lost when we
remember that, in the future re-incarnation of souls, no
memory of the previous life seems to be passed on; so that
the dung beetle's life is not disfigured by memories of his
previous career as, say, the Governor of Texas. In the East
the main motive is longing for the release that transcends
samsara. This is possible because within the constraints of
karma we have the spiritual freedom to move upwards or
downwards. Life is an opportunity to make progress; it is
a journey through many lives, in which we are gradually
moving towards our final liberation. In the language of the

Gita: 'The man of discipline (yogi) makes a serious effort. He becomes pure. After a number of births, perfected, he reaches the highest goal.'[5] Within the Hindu picture of the universe there are many hells as well as many heavens. But these are not the same as the heaven and hell of the Western monotheisms. They are levels of existence on which souls spend limited periods of time.[6]

Though it was the Hebrew Scriptures that supplied Christianity with the elements that were to be developed into the fully articulated concept of hell as eternal punishment, Judaism itself did not go in this direction. In fact, the life of the world to come was not an original emphasis in Judaism. Though there was an evolution towards a belief in the resurrection from the dead, it was always hotly disputed. Readers of the New Testament will remember the controversy between Pharisees, who did, and Sadducees, who did not, believe in the resurrection of the dead.

Unlike Hinduism and Buddhism, in Judaism, Christianity and Islam we only get one shot at life, and the way we live it determines our fate after death. This sense is probably now stronger in contemporary Islam than in either Judaism or Christianity, which have both been heavily influenced by the Enlightenment. But in Islam it is not so much personal sin that leads to hell as a complete rejection of God. We find in Islam the same tolerance of other ways that we find in Judaism and the religions of the East. It is not the rejection of the Qur'an that leads to damnation, because many people have not received it, but the rejection of the God whose nature has been announced by a long succession of prophets. The Qur'an states that: 'Never has there been a community to which an admonisher has not been sent.'[7]

The variety of approaches to the afterlife revealed by this swift survey demonstrates that it would be absurd to imagine that at some stage in human evolution a consortium of spiritual leaders got together and invented the myth of hell in the West, and karma in the East, to act as a deterrent against human wickedness. But it is fairly obvious that there has to be a solid connection between a frustrated sense of moral outrage, particularly in religious bodies, and the evolution of the doctrine. The wicked ought to be punished, but rarely are in this life, so they will have to be punished in the next, because righteousness must be vindicated. It is the thought of the millennia of unrequited suffering that is the strongest emotional element in the logic of punishment after death, though this is, morally speaking, light years away from the terroristic use of the threat of hell to deter young boys from sexual experimentation that so disfigures later developments of the doctrine. 'Surely', the original logic must have reasoned, 'if there is anything for us beyond death, a righteous God must require the wicked to pay for their evil deeds in this life, and repent of them.' Repentance, the change of mind that owns the truth about itself, requires some sort of response on our part, some sort of reparation. A good modern example of this widespread conviction is provided by programmes that bring offenders and their victims together. Often, the encounter leads offenders to a change of awareness about their conduct, and a recognition of the victim as a person. Repentance means a change of attitude, a turning towards and an owning of the truth about oneself.

But what if repentance has not happened in this life? Is there another chance beyond death, supposing that anything awaits us beyond death? The absolute systems say a definite No to that. That is why death-bed repentances feature so strongly in history. It is cutting it fine to leave it till the moment of death, and that is why the old Prayer Book litany prayed fervently against dying 'suddenly and unprepared'. However, there was an interesting development in Roman Catholic theology that modified the rigour of Christian thought on eternal punishment. One of the fascinating things about Catholic theology is the way it invents unpleasant doctrines because of its passion for logic and law, and then gradually admits to itself that it has probably gone too far. So it proceeds to construct ameliorating exceptions to the general rule, into which it manages to fit most people; or it develops the offensive concept in different directions, to give it a saving versatility. This is what happened in the case of hell. As we have already seen, the doctrine that even unbaptised babies went to hell was later slightly modified by the invention of limbo. In a later piece of infernal town planning, purgatory was created. Purgatory was not so much a suburb of hell as a completely new town, midway between heaven and hell. In purgatory the soul confronted what evil it had committed in life, and went through a refining fire that purged and purified it, so that it could at last enter the presence of God in heaven. Banishment to hell was still the verdict for people who died in unrepented mortal sin, while purgatory was for venial sins; but casuistry did allow a bit of leeway, and concepts like invincible ignorance were useful ways of getting reduced sentences even for mortal sinners.

Even if we dismiss this whole scheme of things, as I do, there are several useful human applications of this rather grisly theme in Christian theology. The main one has to be the need to take personal responsibility for our own actions, especially for the pain and damage we have inflicted on others. The important thing to notice here is not any forensic or legal logic: we are not talking about punishment to satisfy the law's demands. That may have its place, but it is not what I am focusing on for the moment. It is important for ourselves to accept responsibility for our actions, and to acknowledge the effect they have had on others, because knowing the truth about ourselves is fundamental to our spiritual and moral development. One of the saddest misuses of a life is to go through it without really getting to know it. Plato said the unexamined life was not worth living. To get through life without any discernible increase in self-knowledge is a terrible waste because it is a refusal to look attentively at the reality that is closest to hand, our own self. That is why all the great systems of spiritual discipline emphasise the importance of self-examination and confession. If we are to grow as humans, we need to know what we are up against within ourselves, need to understand the reality of our condition, our weaknesses, and our strengths, our failures, as well as the things we have done well. Unfortunately, human males, in particular, have developed among themselves cultures of honour and shame, in which losing face or owning up to weakness is not done. This is why it can be particularly difficult to bring them to deep self-awareness, which may be one reason why institutional religion has manufactured brutal spiritual mechanisms, such as hell, in order to blast through the carapace of male insensitivity. Unfortunately, their effect has often been to coarsen rather than refine the process of true spiritual awareness.

But let me return to the concept of hell itself. The idea, as expressed in the sermon from Joyce, or others I could quote, is so gross that something deep and archetypal must be going on below the overt need to control human waywardness by literally scaring the hell out of them. Why did the concept develop in the way it did, with its cast list of demons commissioned to lure unwary souls into their clutches? Paul Tillich gave some thought to this. He believed that the idea of the demonic was the mythical expression of an important human reality, namely, the structural, and therefore inescapable, power of evil. There is a type of mind – kindly, liberal, humanist – that either refuses to, or is incapable of, confronting the intractability of this kind of evil. It sees only 'individual acts of evil, dependent on the free decisions of the conscious personality', it believes 'in the possibility of inducing the great majority of individuals to follow the demands of an integrated personal and social life by education, persuasion, and adequate institutions' says Tillich.[8] This kindly belief in progress and human perfectibility was destroyed by the horrible wars and purges of the twentieth century, as well as by our explorations into the depths of our own psyches. The great analysts of humanity's sick soul, Freud, Jung and Adler, explored and recorded their encounters with destructive forces deep within us that unpredictably determined the energies of individuals and whole groups. It was as though, through their encounter with the unconscious forces within us, they were being offered a preview of the great horrors that were to erupt on the conscious surface of history.

The wars and persecutions of the twentieth century, as well as some of its most exciting intellectual discoveries, have forced us to confront two almost ungovernable sources of evil, which Tillich called the demonic. One is the hidden continent within our own nature that we call the unconscious; and the other is the herd instinct, the collective dimension of humanity that can take over or possess our individuality. These demonic forces, together or separately, can create structures of evil that are beyond the influence of the normal powers of personal good will. They promote individual and social tragedy of the sort that we witnessed throughout the last century, and which we continue to observe helplessly in the genocide and civil strife that disfigure the present. Our impotence in the face of this kind of structured evil, our recognition that the institutions we create have a collective dynamic that often overrides the ethics of the individual, and our experience of the brutal reality of the group mind, all persuade us that there are systems of evil that are superhuman in their power and imperviousness to human rationality. That is why it is difficult to find a way of explaining these great forces that does not fall back on the vocabulary of the supernatural. The best analogy I can think of comes from the kind of weather systems that can make life in the United States dangerously unpredictable and which seem to be increasingly frequent in Britain. The great hurricanes and twisters that wreak such damage on human settlements could easily lead the uneducated mind to supernatural conclusions. Science, however, knows about the collision of weather systems that generates these spectacular forces, and can even predict them. The myth of the demonic is a way of expressing the eruptions and collisions of evil and suffering that so disfigure our history. If it is hell we are thinking of, then we have confronted it in our own time in a series of monstrous evils that might have been scripted by Dante. And none was worse or more archetypal than the holocaust, the destruction of six million Jews in the death camps of Europe. It was as if the hell of the Christian imagination had finally erupted into history and established itself in our midst.

I have already quoted from what I consider to be the greatest of the novels about the holocaust, *The Last of the Just*, by André Schwarz-Bart. I quoted from the passage in which Ernie Levy is in a box car on his way to Auschwitz, shepherding a group of Jewish children. He has consoled them with the lie that they are on their way to the peace and safety of the Kingdom of Israel. When they reach Auschwitz, Ernie leads his little flock into the gas chamber: 'Breathe deeply, my lambs, and quickly' he says. Then we read these unbearable words:

> When the layers of gas had covered everything, there was silence in the dark sky of the room for perhaps a minute, broken only by shrill, racking coughs and the gasps of those too far gone in their agonies to offer a devotion. And first as a stream, then a cascade, then an irrepressible, majestic torrent, the poem which, through the smoke of fires and above the funeral pyres of history, the Jews – who for two thousand years never bore arms and never had either missionary empires or coloured slaves – the old love poem which the Jews traced in letters of blood on the earth's hard crust unfurled in the gas chamber, surrounded it, dominated its dark, abysmal sneer: 'SHEMA ISRAEL. ADONAI ELOHENU ADONAI EH'HOTH ... Hear O Israel, the Eternal our God, the Eternal is One. O Lord by your grace you nourish the living, and by your great pity you resurrect the dead; and you uphold the weak, cure the sick, break the chains of slaves; and faithfully you keep your promises to those who sleep in the dust. Who is like unto you, O merciful Father, and who could be like unto you?'

The voices died one by one along the unfinished poem; the dying children had already dug their nails into Ernie's thighs, and Golda's embrace was already weaker, her kisses were blurred, when suddenly she clung fiercely to her beloved's neck and whispered hoarsely: 'Then I'll never see you again? Never again?'

Ernie managed to spit up the needle of fire jabbing at his throat and, as the girl's body slumped against him, its eyes wide in the opaque night, he shouted against her unconscious ear, 'In a little while, I swear it!' . . . And then he knew that he could do nothing more for anyone in the world, and in the flash that preceded his own annihilation he remembered, happily, the legend of Rabbi Chanina ben Teradion, as Mordecai had joyfully recited it: when the gentle rabbi, wrapped in the scrolls of the Torah, was flung upon the pyre by the Romans for having taught the law, and when they lit the faggots, branches still green to make his torture last, his pupils said, Master, what do you see? And Rabbi Chanina answered, I see the parchment burning, but the letters are taking wing . . . Ah, yes, surely, the letters are taking wing, Ernie repeated as the flame blazing in his chest suddenly invaded his brain. With dying arms he embraced Golda's body in an already unconscious gesture of loving protection, and they were found in this position half-an-hour later by the team of Sonderkommando responsible for burning the Jews in the crematory ovens. And so it was for millions, who from Luftmensch became Luft. I shall not translate. So this story will not finish with some tomb to be visited in pious memory. For the smoke that rises from crematoria obeys physical laws like any other: the particles come together and disperse according to the wind, which propels them. The only pilgrimage, dear reader, would be to look sadly at a stormy sky now and then.

The novel ends:

At times, it is true, one's heart could break in sorrow.

> But often too, preferably in the evening, I cannot help
> thinking that Ernie Levy, dead six million times, is still
> alive, somewhere, I don't know where . . . Yesterday, as
> I stood in the street trembling in despair, rooted to the
> spot, a drop of pity fell from above my face; but there
> was no breeze in the air, no cloud in the sky . . . there
> was only a presence.[9]

I make no apology for that long quotation, because it
encapsulates the evil we are capable of inflicting on one
another. More significantly, it shows that hell exists, not
in some supernatural sphere, not in our imagination, but
in actual human history. Hell, a largely Christian development, was built on earth, in our time, as a crematory
for the Jews. Why has the Christian world hated Jews so
much? We could trace the trajectory of that hatred from
the Gospel of John that found 'the Jews' guilty of the death
of Christ, through the pogroms of the Middle Ages, to
the Final Solution. Among other things, that trajectory
demonstrates the demonic use to which the Bible can be
put: Matthew's gospel fatefully puts these words into the
mouths of the crowd that called for the death of Jesus:
'His blood be on us and on our children,' and it has been
down the centuries, rivers of it. There is something of the
demonic here, something beyond explanation, something
right off the trajectory of history. Why this hatred of
the Jews?

The best guess I have discovered is a thought from
George Steiner, who is also obsessed with the question.
In several places in his writings, and most recently in his
autobiography, *Errata*, he wonders if humanity does not
hate the Jewish people because it bore the law to them,
and the pain of conscience. In Moses, Jesus and Marx, he
suggests, the Jew has confronted the human conscience

with an impossible demand. The moral commandments which come through Moses are uncompromising, and 'entail the mutation of common man. We are to discipline soul and flesh into perfection. We are to outgrow our own shadow.'[10] Steiner continues his paraphrase, 'Cease being what you are, what biology and circumstance have made you. Become, at a fearful price of abnegation, what you could be.' According to Steiner, 'This is the first of the three moments of transcendent imposition on man out of Judaism.' The second comes from Jesus. 'He requires of men and women an altruism, a counter-instinctual, "unnatural" restraint towards all who do us injury and offence.' Steiner continues, 'The profoundly natural impulse to avenge injustice, oppression and deri-sion do have their place in the house of Israel. A refusal to forget injury or humiliation can warm the heart. Christ's ordinance of total love, of self-offering to the assailant, is, in any strict sense, an enormity. The victim is to love his butcher. A monstrous proposition. But one shedding fathomless light. How are mortal men and women to fulfil it?'[11]

What Steiner calls 'the third knock on the door' comes from Karl Marx, who secularises 'the messianic logic of social justice, of Edenic plenty for all, of peace on an undivided earth'.[12] He goes on to talk about Marx's rage against social inequality, against the sterile cruelty of wealth, against unnecessary famine and *misère*. He concludes, 'Three times, Judaism has brought Western civilisation face to face with the blackmail of the ideal. What graver affront?'[13] These morally towering figures are uncomfortable for most of us to live with because they challenge our compromises, our corruptions, our failure to struggle for the ideal, the absolute. They fill us with guilt and shame; and guilt and shame easily turn to self-hatred; and, since self-hatred cannot live with itself, it goes in search of a scapegoat. We kill the consciences of history and create hell on earth.

CHAPTER EIGHT

Get Out of Jail Free

In chapter four I referred to Thomas Kuhn's ground-breaking essay, *The Structure of Scientific Revolutions*, and his persuasive insight that science was human and that shifts in scientific thinking, paradigm shifts, are prompted by social forces as well as by what we might think of as pure science. This should not surprise us, of course, but it is worth repeating because one of the permanent fallacies we commit in all the human disciplines is to accord them a clinical objectivity they cannot have. So the ideal scientific experiment is one that is completely clinical and abstracted, conducted from some kind of bunker that insulates the scientist from outside influences. No such isolation is possible or desirable. There is no way we can get ourselves out of our skin or out of our social and cultural context. Even a scientist as rigorous as Darwin, in finding a narrative in which to express his discoveries, had to use metaphors that clearly came from nineteenth-century capitalism and its notion of struggle and the survival of the fittest.

If non-scientific factors contribute to the work of science, then it is certainly the case that non-theological factors contribute to the work of theology. I would go further and say that there are no such things as purely theological factors. There may be objective elements in theology such as revelations and historical debates over them, but the work of theology is an inescapably human work. In addition to the human factors involved, scientists do have an external reality to work on and look at in the form of everything other than themselves that exists. Theologians, in spite of the claims they make to the contrary, do not have access to an equivalent metaphysical reality from which they can make deductions and conduct experiments. Everything they have to deal with comes from within the human envelope. Theology is really another aspect of psychology, another way of describing human experience and its struggles with itself. The proof of this, as we have seen, is that, even if we assert the existence of a reality other than ourselves which invades us and reveals itself to us, we are inescapably fixed on the human end of that experience and cannot know the Other as it is in itself, but only as we receive it or have known it. The reason theological dispute is so endless is that there are no empirical experiments we can appeal to that can obviously settle them, the way we might settle a dispute over the exact temperature of the boiling point of water. This can only disturb us if we have persuaded ourselves that when we are doing theology we are dealing with a substance other than ourselves. Whereas the enduringly fascinating thing about theology is that it provides us with a mirror into our own souls. This is particularly the case when we come to examine one of the most fascinating and complex of the Christian theological themes, the idea of Justification by Faith.

In John Osborne's play about Martin Luther, the German reformer, he links Luther's constipation to his discovery of the significance of the theme of Justification by Faith in Paul's Letter to the Romans. W.H. Auden made the same point when he said that 'Revelation came to Luther in the privy.'[1] In Osborne's play the release of the great idea that ignited the Reformation exactly coincides with a massive evacuation of Luther's bowels. Luther's anguish was caused by the fact that he felt incapable of achieving the perfection God required of him. Many of the great religious geniuses have been souls in torment about themselves who found peace through the discovery of a spiritual truth that rescued them from despair. Buddhism is one of the most attractive examples of how human anguish can prompt people to the search for a costly peace. Launched twenty-five centuries ago in northern India by Siddartha Guatama, it offers a way of salvation or escape from the tedious repetitions of *samsara*. The story is well known of the young prince who renounced worldly glory to seek salvation, and discovered that the stumbling block to his own salvation, and the cause of all human misery, was desire or craving. If he could get rid of that desire, banish that craving, he would know the peace of high Nirvana. The genius of Buddhism is that it is a Middle Way that repudiates two extremes, the worthless life of self-indulgence and the equally worthless life of self-torture. The difference between Buddhism and Christianity is that Buddhism is essentially a practice, an arduous discipline that can deliver peace and compassion to its adherents. Christianity also has its spiritual disciplines, but it has never been able to divest itself of the belief that its doctrines are themselves saving and life-changing. Much of this goes back to the originating genius of Christian theology, Saul of Tarsus who became Paul. The paradox is that what was for Paul a liberating psychological experience was later to be hardened into a formula that radically contradicted his original insight and the experience that prompted it.

It is hazardous to guess at the psychological disposition of long-dead people who are only known to us through their writing, but Paul did provide us with a lot of material for our speculations because he disclosed much of himself in a series of letters that are a valuable tool for our exercise in detection. The American psychologist and philosopher William James divided people into healthy and sick souls, into people with equable dispositions and people who are internally conflicted and divided. Paul seems to have been an example of the latter. He tells us in the Letter to the Romans that he is puzzled by the divisions in his own nature:

> [15] I do not understand my own actions. For I do not do what I want, but I do the very thing I hate. [16] Now if I do what I do not want, I agree that the law is good. [17] But in fact it is no longer I that do it, but sin that dwells within me. [18] For I know that nothing good dwells within me, that is, in my flesh. I can will what is right, but I cannot do it. [19] For I do not do the good I want, but the evil I do not want is what I do. [20] Now if I do what I do not want, it is no longer I that do it, but sin that dwells within me.
>
> [21] So I find it to be a law that when I want to do what is good, evil lies close at hand. [22] For I delight in the law of God in my inmost self, [23] but I see in my members another law at war with the law of my mind, making me captive to the law of sin that dwells in my members. [24] Wretched man that I am! Who will rescue me from this body of death?[2]

The normal way to interpret Paul's personal anguish is to say that he sought to make himself perfect through the minute observance of the Torah or holiness code of the Jewish people. He tells us in the Letter to the Galations that he was a strict practitioner of the way of his people:

[13] You have heard, no doubt, of my earlier life in Judaism. I was violently persecuting the church of God and was trying to destroy it. [14] I advanced in Judaism beyond many among my people of the same age, for I was far more zealous for the traditions of my ancestors.[3]

An insight from Rabbi Lionel Blue may help us here. In a lecture he gave in Edinburgh in January 2000 he remarked on the different ways that people of the three great monotheistic religions go mad. In Judaism it tends to take the form of obsessive-compulsive neurosis; in Christianity it becomes sado-masochism; and in Islam it is megalomania. It is a perceptive insight. There can be little doubt that the Christian obsession with guilt and punishment has been richly productive of sado-masochism in the practices of its adherents, as well as in its iconography. Obsessive-compulsive neurosis is an equally obvious danger for those who follow a highly ritualised religious code. And Woody Allen is a good example of how these tendencies can be entirely secularised. As far as Islam is concerned, there does seem to be a tendency to megalomania, if only in response to what is perceived to be international prejudice against this ancient religion.

If there is anything in Lionel Blue's insight, it might help to account for Paul's crisis, both before and after his conversion. We do not know if he ever met or heard Jesus and he certainly does not quote him nor show explicit acquaintance with his teaching. What he does is to develop a mystical response to the crucifixion of Jesus, but at its heart there does seem to be a relieved acceptance of Jesus' critique of code-based religion because it can become a vehicle for obsessive-compulsive neurosis. One of the themes in the life of Jesus was his attitude to the Sabbath, which exemplified his approach to various fundamental matters. We invent systems, such as days of rest, to help us to live wisely, but there is a tendency in us to take these useful inventions too seriously and offer them an absolute allegiance. One of the controversies that Jesus got into with the legalists of his day was precisely over this issue.

[6:1] One sabbath while Jesus was going through the grainfields, his disciples plucked some heads of grain, rubbed them in their hands, and ate them. [2] But some of the Pharisees said, 'Why are you doing what is not lawful on the sabbath?' [3] Jesus answered, 'Have you not read what David did when he and his companions were hungry: [4] He entered the house of God and took and ate the bread of the Presence, which it is not lawful for any but the priests to eat, and gave some to his companions.' [5] Then he said to them, 'The Son of Man is lord of the sabbath.'

[6] On another sabbath he entered the synagogue and taught, and there was a man there whose right hand was withered. [7] The scribes and the Pharisees watched him to see whether he would cure on the sabbath, so that they might find an accusation against him. [8] Even though he knew what they were thinking, he said to the man who had the withered hand, 'Come and stand here.' He got up and stood there. [9] Then Jesus said to them, 'I ask you, is it lawful to do good or to do harm on the sabbath, to save life or to destroy it?' [10] After looking around at all of them, he said to him, 'Stretch out your hand.' He did so, and his hand was restored. [11] But they were filled with fury and discussed with one another what they might do to Jesus.[4]

Mark's original version of the first of these two incidents

is even more significant because it contains the saying that relativises all human systems, including religious ones, and refuses them any absolute right. They are all essentially human and therefore provisional in their usefulness. The time may come when they have to be modified in response to a particular human need, as in the case of the man with the withered arm in Luke, or replaced entirely by a system that does the job better.

> [23] One sabbath he was going through the grainfields; and as they made their way his disciples began to pluck heads of grain. [24] The Pharisees said to him, 'Look, why are they doing what is not lawful on the sabbath?' [25] And he said to them, 'Have you never read what David did when he and his companions were hungry and in need of food? [26] He entered the house of God, when Abiathar was high priest, and ate the bread of the Presence, which it is not lawful for any but the priests to eat, and he gave some to his companions.' [27] Then he said to them, 'The sabbath was made for humankind, and not humankind for the sabbath.'[5]

Our danger is that we often make the things we invent so absolute that they end up defeating the purpose they were intended to serve. There's an amusing example of this in the film *Meet the Parents*. The hero, played by Ben Stiller, is in an airport departure lounge about to board his plane. The steward calls for passengers in seat-rows nine and above to come forward. Since the departure lounge is empty, our hero steps forward and presents his boarding card for seat-row eight. The steward orders him to step back because his row has not been called. He remonstrates with her: 'No one else is boarding, why can't I come through?' 'Because we board by strict rotation of seat-row' is the reply. They wait for a few minutes while no one boards; then she calls for all remaining passengers to come forward and he, alone, presents his ticket. Boarding planes by seat-row rotation makes sense, it assists us in wise living, but to make it an absolute rule in all circumstances is insane. That's the point, the only point in Jesus' dispute about the Sabbath. Exact, compulsive observance of the letter of any code can take us over and drive us mad, as we seek to achieve a perfect conformity to the law or custom.

Whatever the precise nature of Paul's religious torment, he found release from it in a particular understanding of the work of Jesus. Paul expressed his discovery in a way that suggested that the work of Jesus effected some kind of mystical change in the order of things and thereby mechanistically changed relations between God and humanity. Behind the formula he used there probably lay an awareness of Jesus' critique of the dangers of code, because it can turn what was meant to assist humanity into a heavy burden round its neck. In Paul's language the liberation he experienced is expressed in the metaphor of justification or acquittal. The tortured, guilty soul is gratuitously acquitted of guilt and set free.

[8:1] There is therefore now no condemnation for those who are in Christ Jesus. [2] For the law of the Spirit of life in Christ Jesus has set you free from the law of sin and of death. [3] For God has done what the law, weakened by the flesh, could not do: by sending his own Son in the likeness of sinful flesh, and to deal with sin, he condemned sin in the flesh, [4] so that the just requirement of the law might be fulfilled in us, who walk not according to the flesh but according to the Spirit.[6]

[118]

I think it is more useful to try to figure out the psychological dynamic in this moment of liberation than to be too painstaking about the theology. The theology, in any case, seems to shift around, as have the theories that have been built upon it. For example, the verses just quoted easily lend themselves to the development of what is called satisfaction theory, which holds that human sinfulness has built up a colossal debt towards God that we are incapable of paying. Christ can be thought of as offering God satisfaction, with the idea swinging between his being punished instead of us and his offering God, finally, a perfect human life. Sometimes Paul switches from the law court to the slave market, from the forensic metaphor of acquittal or justification to the metaphor of redemption. Slaves could be freed in a number of ways, including being paid for or bought out by a redeemer, the way that, on Friday night when the pay packet came in, the poor redeemed items they had pawned on Wednesday, when there was no money in the house. The precise meaning of the metaphors aside, what is beyond dispute is that something radical and liberating happened to Paul which brought him charging into the Christian movement. He associated his liberation with the death and resurrection of Jesus rather than, explicitly, with his teaching. Implicitly, however, there is present in the theology of Paul an association between his own liberation from religious compulsions and the life and work of Jesus.

In his turn, Luther was to achieve a similar catharsis. He seems to have been another sick soul, earnestly searching for an elusive perfection through monastic observance. We left him in the monastery privy, meditating on Paul's Letter to the Romans. He could not get himself out of the predicament he was in. By definition, he was his own

problem: he was a sinner, incapable of achieving righteousness and the spiritual peace it would bring. Instead,
the struggle for perfection brought torment. He knew the
law was righteous, but he was foul, unable to find peace
by following it. Who would rescue him from this captivity?
It was the same question that Paul asked and he received
the same answer: what he could not achieve by his own
efforts was freely made available to him by the grace of
Christ. Standing in the dock, guilty as charged, waiting to
hear the sentence of death, he is staggered to hear the
words of acquittal from the judge that let him out of jail
free with no penalty. Another has paid the fine, served
the sentence, changed the heart of the judge: pick your
metaphor. We get the result, the verdict, but what we do
not get from either Paul or Luther is a real understanding
of the psychological revolution within their own hearts.
We get the formula they used to express the catharsis they
had experienced, the conclusion of the drama, but we are
not let in on how it was psychologically worked out within
them. If we can look at another sick soul who went through
similar torments we might get a clearer picture of what was
going on.

Paul Tillich was another troubled religious genius. He
struggled unsuccessfully against compulsive sexual relationships that today would have had him driven from the
American university scene. We do not have to guess at the
effect this struggle had upon his own inner life, because
he has told us in his own words in a famous sermon on a
verse from Paul's Letter to the Romans, 5.20: 'Moreover
the law entered, that the offence might abound. But where
sin abounded, grace did much more abound.' For Tillich,
in this sermon, the concept of sin is about separation. We
experience sin as something that tears us away from our

best sense of ourselves, from those we love and from God. This, according to Tillich, was Paul's experience: 'In the picture of Jesus as the Christ, which appeared to him at the moment of his greatest separation from other men, from himself and God, he found himself accepted in spite of his being rejected. And when he found that he was accepted, he was able to accept himself and to be reconciled to others.'[7] The title of Tillich's sermon is 'You are accepted' and there can be little doubt that we are looking in on his agonised struggles with his own nature and its compulsions. He uses the phrase 'struck by grace' to capture the justifying moment, the moment that tells us we are accepted in spite of everything we know against ourselves. He writes:

> Do we know what it means to be struck by grace? It does *not* mean that we suddenly believe that God exists, or that Jesus is the Saviour, or that the Bible contains the truth. Grace strikes us when we are in great pain and restlessness. It strikes us when we walk through the dark valley of a meaningless and empty life. It strikes us when we feel that our separation is deeper than usual, because we have violated another life, a life which we loved, or from which we were estranged. It strikes us when our disgust for our own being, our indifference, our weakness, our hostility, and our lack of direction and composure have become intolerable to us. It strikes us when, year after year, the longed-for perfection of life does not appear, when the old compulsions reign within us as they have for decades, when despair destroys all joy and courage.[8]

In this raw and honest passage, Tillich has laid bare the struggles with self-hatred that characterise many troubled souls. And it is precisely at the moment of deepest help-lessness, when we have given up the pretence that we are other than we are and are not likely to change, that the moment of grace comes, the moment Paul and Luther associated with the work of Jesus, but a moment that comes in many ways to many different people in many different places. It is the moment of acceptance or justification.

This is how Tillich puts it:

Sometimes at that moment a wave of light breaks into our darkness, and it is as though a voice were saying: 'You are accepted. *You are accepted*, accepted by that which is greater than you, and the name of which you do not know. Do not ask for the name now; perhaps you will find it later; do not try to do anything now; perhaps later you will do much. Do not seek for anything; do not intend anything. *Simply accept the fact that you are accepted!*' If that happens to us, we experience grace. We may not be better than before, and we may not believe more than before. But everything is transformed. In that moment, grace conquers sin, and reconciliation bridges the gulf of estrangement. And nothing is demanded of this experience, no religious or moral or intellectual presupposition, nothing but *acceptance*.[9]

In this passage Tillich found the words to convey a liberating human experience that should be more frequent than it is, the moment not of rueful self-acceptance, but of joyful self-acceptance, almost of love of the self. We are well aware today of the kinks and twists in our nature. There is, for instance, the scape-goat phenomenon or what psychologists call 'projective identification' which, if undetected and unadmitted, can be so deadly. Nietzsche captures it perfectly in the *Genealogy of Morals*: 'Every sufferer instinctively seeks a cause for his suffering; more exactly, an agent; still more specifically, a guilty agent who is susceptible to suffering – in short, some living thing upon which he can, on some pretext or other, vent his affects, actually or in effigy: for the venting of his affects represents the greatest attempt on the part of the suffering to win relief, *anaesthesia*, the narcotic he cannot help desiring to deaden pain of any kind.'[10]

There is an ugly example of this in the film *American Beauty* in the person of the tough, manly, fascist American Marine Captain who lives next door to the Kevin Spacey character. It is obvious that the tightly coiled soldier is a deeply conflicted person, whose self-hatred shows itself in violence towards his son and contempt of anything approaching liberal or hippie values. His son is supplying the Spacey character with the happy weed marijuana, but the captain thinks their relationship is sexual. Convinced that Spacey is gay, he makes a pass at him and is gently rebuffed. Unable to live with the truth that has just been revealed, he kills the man he has just tried to make love to. He kills in his neighbour what he cannot live with in his own nature.

Homophobia is not the only example of this phenomenon, but it is an extremely powerful one, particularly in religious institutions. There is no sadder figure in Christianity than the self-hating gay priest, often allied to reactionary movements that stand for virulent opposition to everything he himself longs for, but refuses to admit. One of the most disfiguring aspects of the Church of England at the moment is the way some members of its gay brigade have become captive to this kind of inversion. During the campaign for the ordination of women in the

Episcopal Church of the US, a close alliance developed between the women's movement and the campaign for gay and lesbian liberation. It was acknowledged that human liberation was indivisible and had to be accepted in total. Self-owning and self-respecting gay men had no difficulty in making alliances with other groups who were victims of prejudice. That did not happen in England, where one of the groups most virulently opposed to women's emancipation was the closeted gay fraternity, many of whom are allied to reactionary movements such as *Forward in Faith*. Divided within themselves, they lead painfully unjustified lives. Justification or grace comes when we fully acknowledge who and what we are. We say the words to ourselves that define our condition, beyond all denial and dishonesty, just as we shall one day have to say Yes to our own dying, another human reality that provokes panic and flight.

There is, I think, an important distinction to be made here. The moment of grace or justification is a moment of self-acceptance, though not necessarily acceptance of everything that we have done. We may have done terrible things and there will be a time when we have to come to terms with that; for the moment, however, it is ourselves we must accept unconditionally: 'This is who I am and I must say Yes to myself.' We have to act towards ourselves like the insanely loving father in the Parable of the Prodigal Son, which is a great story of grace and justification. We can still hope and pray that one day we might change and be all the things we long to be, but for now there is only this moment of grace, this moment in which we must run to meet ourselves as we trudge away from the far country of self-hatred and say Yes to ourselves. And all of this is consistent with public exposure of our shame, with imprisonment, with the loss of those we love: in the depth of our hearts we have to accept ourselves utterly. We must remember here what Tillich says about not seeking or intending anything other than the moment of self-acceptance. The way I would put it is to say that this moment of grace and justification must not be submitted to for prudential or instrumental reasons, in order to lever change into our lives to bring them up to the required standard. There must be no ulterior motive. The moment of grace and justification has to be absolute and single, bearing only its own meaning and integrity. Even on the scaffold I must be able to say an absolute Yes to this self that is the gratuitous mystery of life in me. To deny that is to deny the closest life gets to me. My life has to be celebrated, utterly accepted. As a matter of fact, however, it seems to follow that people who have made this peace with themselves do seem able to live more peacefully and tolerantly with others. You can tell the edgy, conflicted souls, because they are likely to be edgy and conflicted with everyone.

Justification is a universal human experience, even though it expresses itself within different contexts and takes on the colour of the particular vessel that contains it. In the Christian tradition it is particularly associated with the life of Jesus. We can find the liberation in the wisdom of his approach to human systems and the way even the best of them can become tyrannical. The Church has done more than that, largely because of the influence of Paul, and has gone on to suggest that the death of Jesus, in particular, was a forensic act that achieved objective ends. This is the mythic vehicle which bears, for Christians, the universal human experience of justifying grace. Unfortunately, what was a particular way of defining a universal experience has turned into its profound limitation. And what was meant to celebrate our freedom only becomes another way of imprisoning us, this time within a theological formula that turns the experience on its head. Paul did genuinely acknowledge that his moment of liberation was a moment of grace, of sheer gratuitous joy that he was accepted. It is a tragic irony that justification, as a theological formula, was later to be turned into a pre-requisite for the acceptance of free grace. What was given freely is expropriated by religious monopolists and doled out to their adherents. It's a confidence trick, however. Air cannot be privatised, nor can grace. And, in our hearts, we all know that.

CHAPTER NINE

The Big Bang

One of the problems people have with Christian beliefs is that they do not know what they are for. They may know what the belief is, but they are not sure what it is meant to do or why it is important to hold it. After all, everyone has beliefs of one sort or another, but people usually understand what they are for and how they work. For example, if a friend is accused of some crime or offence, they say, 'I believe in Simon and I know he is incapable of an act like that.' A belief of this sort is an act of trust, a conviction about the character of another person that you act upon. And it can be tested, it can be verified or falsified. In the case of Simon, who may have been accused of embezzling funds from the charity of which he is treasurer, there is a solid chance that his innocence will be proved or his guilt established. If he is declared innocent, our trust in him, our belief in his honesty, will be vindicated; if he is proved guilty, our trust in him will be broken. Whatever happens to it, we at least know what our belief in Simon is about and we know what it would take to vindicate or destroy it.

So there is a logic behind belief in people, which we can all understand: it is about placing our trust in them, sometimes in a risky way. Trust is important in day-to-day living. We can't spend our time constantly testing the honesty and the trustworthiness of our friends, so we go on our intuitions, our hunches about them, our experience, the knowledge we have built up about them over the years. That kind of trust is the reality that undergirds all our important relationships. Come to think of it, it is the basis of almost every aspect of our lives: many of the things we do are based on assumptions that are acts of trust or belief. Apart from trusting our friends, we put our trust in surgeons when we have an operation – that's a very radical sort of trust, because we allow them to anaesthetise us and cut us open and mess about with our insides. Less momentously, we trust the transport system. When I get on the train at Edinburgh for King's Cross, I believe that I'll be taken to London, not Lowestoft. All these cases, though they are examples of belief, are based on experience, experience of the trustworthiness of the Health Service or the railway company, so that I am prepared to put myself in their hands for a heart operation or a trip to London.

But how do religious beliefs operate, how do they work? There seem to be two difficulties with them. First of all, it is not easy either to falsify or to verify them. We can take steps to verify Simon's honesty; we can test the trustworthiness of a surgeon by various means, including the number of people who leave his operating theatre alive rather than dead; and we can study the claims made by the train companies about how many of their trains made it to London on time last year. How do we verify the existence of God, or even falsify it, for that matter? You can get round that difficulty, to some extent, by saying you choose to trust your intuition, or you are persuaded by the philosophical arguments that deal with the matter, or you have decided to bet on the possibility, following Pascal on the grounds that if you win you win everything, and if you lose you only lose nothing. Pascal's wager is superficially seductive, but on closer analysis it leaves lots of questions. What God are we betting on? If you have followed my argument so far, I hope you will admit that our understanding of God and God's role in the life of the universe has shifted radically over the centuries. So on what understanding of God are we going to bet? If believing in God is to hold in our minds the conviction that there is a superhuman being to whom we give the name God, it is still legitimate to ask: 'So what? What difference does it make?' After all, according to the Letter of James, even 'the devils believe, and tremble'.[1] So it is entirely appropriate to ask this other question of belief: 'What's the point, what difference does it make, what is its cash value?', to use an expression from William James.

If we think of miracles, for instance, which many people proudly claim to believe in, as though some special virtue were attached to such a belief, what difference does it make to believe in them? Leaving aside for the moment whether Jesus actually performed any, what would be the point in believing that he did, what would the belief be for? In an earlier period of theological history, people used Jesus' miracles in a practical way as evidence of his divinity, but that is a perilous enterprise for us to engage in today and few apologists for orthodox Christianity proffer it in serious debate. Apart from the healing miracles, which can be made to fit our understanding of the psychosomatic nature of the human being, most interpreters now allocate the miracles of Jesus to the world-view of his time and accord them little significance in the lives of modern believers.

After all, miracles of the sort described in the New Testament continue to occur, but not where we live and rarely to people like us. If a statue starts weeping in Sicily or an impression of the face of Jesus appears in the sky above a motel in El Paso, supernatural claims are made for them, and large crowds gather, but most of us will look for natural explanations for the events, including straightforward fraud. It does not follow, however, that we will want to dismiss as primitive or ignorant those who believe in a supernatural cause for these events. We understand well enough that people have always occupied different places in their understanding of things. I cannot grudge those who believe in a magical world-view the comfort or excitement of holding that view; but I cannot hold it myself, not because I am a representative of faithless scepticism, but because I have inherited a different way of looking at things and it would be dishonest of me to abandon it or exclude religion from its consequential effects. In this area, we have to pick our way through a defile between cultural arrogance and superiority, on the one hand, and honest acceptance of our own cognitive situation, on the other. The miraculous way of looking at things is still held by some people with perfect integrity today, just as it was once possible to hold an honest belief in Ptolemaic astronomy. But once a particular society has shifted to a different scheme of interpretation, a different paradigm of understanding, why is it held to be virtuous or faithful to cleave to remnants of the old world-view in our religious understanding? I can appreciate the argument from preference or cultural weariness here, rather than the claim of faithfulness. Some people just don't like new things: they prefer stage coaches to steam trains, ocean liners to jumbo jets, coal fires to central heating. It is not difficult to sympathise with this kind of weariness with change and the endless flux of history. When we encounter this kind of nostalgia among our friends, we smile, shrug our shoulders and say something to the effect that James is just a young fogey who doesn't like the modern world. All of that we can negotiate and even appreciate as having a certain kind of counter-cultural attractiveness to it. The stakes shoot up when we enter the religious end of the argument. People might prefer steam trains to diesels for romantic reasons, but it would be wrong of them to claim the virtue of faithfulness for doing so. They are exercising a preference, that's all. We might offer a similarly relaxed attitude to people who said that they preferred the religious world-view of earlier societies to the scientific world-view of their own; or that they liked the drama and unexpectedness of the medieval consciousness, with its sense of encircling spiritual forces out to infest and entrap the unwary human; and they might even persuade themselves that they were inhabiting it. Of course, we know that they are incapable of entering the consciousness of a French peasant of a thousand years ago; and if they pulled off the trick it would probably scare them witless. These are games we play, choices we make; and it is all right, as long as we don't exert spiritual blackmail on those who choose not to play the game.

The point is that the scheme of interpretation that presents Jesus as a visitant from a supernatural realm who performed wonders, including raising the dead and walking on the water of the Sea of Galilee, is just that: a scheme of interpretation, a way of responding to events that was congruent with a particular stage of understanding and development. In that world, people regularly witnessed miracles, encountered ghosts, were infested by demons and knew of men who had been turned into wolves during the full moon. That was how most people interpreted what was happening around them. David Hume understood what was going on:

> We are placed in this world, as in a great theatre, where the true springs and causes of every event are entirely concealed from us; nor have we either sufficient wisdom to foresee, or power to prevent those ills, with which we are continually threatened. We hang in perpetual suspense between life and death, health and sickness, plenty and want; which are distributed amongst the human species by secret and unknown causes, whose operation is oft unexpected, and always unaccountable. These *unknown causes*, then, become the constant object of our hope and fear; and while the passions are kept in perpetual alarm by an anxious expectation of the events, the imagination is equally employed in forming ideas of those powers, on which we have so entire a dependence.'[2]

What Hume called our 'ideas of those powers, on which we have so entire a dependence' have been in permanent flux, as the history of our species, including its ideas, so clearly illustrates. If we are wise, we won't sneer at earlier ideas about the powers that control us, but nor will we accord them virtue just because they came before us. Apart from school boards in the buckle of the Bible Belt in the USA, most people in our world accept the narrative metaphor of evolution as the best way of accounting for things on planet earth. Who knows, a better way of stating the situation may come along, but most of us operate within the Darwinian paradigm fairly successfully today. What, then, is the point of insisting that the now abandoned paradigm of Creationism is true? Why is it held to be virtuous to go on *believing* it, or any of the other elements from previous ways of explaining things? The immediate reason is that in religious discourse we have accorded a particularly privileged status to the documents that narrate the old paradigm. The traditional way of putting this is to say they are 'inspired' or dictated by God and are therefore deemed to be beyond correction. We have already noticed the circularity of this argument: we believe the Bible, because it tells us that it is the word of God and God cannot be wrong. A deeper reason for holding to a previous understanding of things is probably rooted in our psychological need for certainty, even if we manufacture the certainty ourselves. We are unhappy with the fluidity and impermanence of the explanations that are around today. Something in us wants more than this kind of experimental provisionality. If we are not careful, this is the kind of need that can seduce us into falling for dictators and their grand schemes, even if they are only American tele-evangelists. There is no doubt that grand, totalising claims can rescue us, for a time, from anguish and *ennui* and make living worthwhile again, but that is why they are so dangerous. When they fail us, usually because we discover more honest ways of understanding the world, we can be left with an utter contempt for all religion.

Let me return to my question. For the sake of argument, let us suppose that we persuaded ourselves to believe in Creationism or that Jesus materially multiplied five small loaves and three small fish into enough food for more than 5,000. Will believing these things make any difference to us or make us better people? Is there some virtue in believing things that accord with a previous world-view precisely because they are contrary to the present state of knowledge in our culture? Is there a believing muscle we exercise by persuading ourselves to entertain fabulous possibilities? Christian doctrinal beliefs are mainly about the interpretation of distant events that are beyond our ability to falsify or verify, so we can't resolve the issue by any obvious test. There seem to be two options for us: we can either get ourselves embroiled in the factual detail of claim and counter-claim; or we can resolve the issue by the paradigm test. We admit that the challenge of Jesus is completely enmeshed in a world-view we can no longer accept, but we decide that its cultural envelope is incidental to its main message, so we can still make use of it today. If we take that approach, then for us a Christian belief is not a device for containing obsolete interpretations of the universe, but an action indicator. This means that Christianity is not an organisation for the reproduction of antique mental furniture, but is a movement that presents a fundamental moral challenge to humanity. Christianity is not a way of explaining the world; it is a way of disturbing the world. So the only test left is the difference a belief makes, the cash value test.

This approach is particularly important when we come to consider the central or constitutive Christian belief, which is the doctrine of the resurrection of Jesus from the dead. At first sight it seems to be an either/or issue: he either rose from the dead or he didn't, so make your choice. However, if the approach I have been adopting has any integrity to it, there is likely to be more to the issue than either persuading ourselves to install an old piece of mental furniture in our minds or rejecting it out of hand without a moment's further thought. We might be persuaded of the physical fact of the resurrection without it making the slightest difference to our actual lives.

Theologians can be quite subtle in talking about the resurrection today. A parallel with the puzzle of the existence of the universe might help here. If the Big

Bang theory is a hypothetical way of accounting for the origin of the universe, we could say that we have no direct access to whatever it was, but only to its effects in a universe that still appears to be expanding. In other words, we read back from the present to the past and put forward our best guess as to what got the universe going. By analogy, we could say that some kind of decisive event got the Christian movement going. Something must have happened to the disciples of Jesus to change them from the demoralised followers of a fallen leader into people of courage who now proclaimed the message of the one they had earlier deserted. The earliest account we have of the resurrection is from Paul, in the First Letter to the Corinthians, chapter 15:

[15:1] Now I would remind you, brothers and sisters, of the good news that I proclaimed to you, which you in turn received, in which also you stand, [2] through which also you are being saved, if you hold firmly to the message that I proclaimed to you – unless you have come to believe in vain.

[3] For I handed on to you as of first importance what I in turn had received: that Christ died for our sins in accordance with the scriptures, [4] and that he was buried, and that he was raised on the third day in accordance with the scriptures, [5] and that he appeared to Cephas, then to the twelve. [6] Then he appeared to more than five hundred brothers and sisters at one time, most of whom are still alive, though some have died. [7] Then he appeared to James, then to all the apostles. [8] Last of all, as to one untimely born, he appeared also to me. [9] For I am the least of the apostles, unfit to be called an apostle, because I persecuted the church of God. [10] But by the grace of God I am what I am, and his grace toward me has not been in vain. On the contrary,

I worked harder than any of them – though it was not I, but the grace of God that is with me. [11] Whether then it was I or they, so we proclaim and so you have come to believe.

In many ways, verse eight is the most significant part of Paul's statement: 'Last of all, as to one untimely born, he appeared also to me.' There are several accounts of Paul's conversion on the road to Damascus, such as the following verses from the Acts of the Apostles.

[9:1] Meanwhile Saul, still breathing threats and murder against the disciples of the Lord, went to the high priest [2] and asked him for letters to the synagogues at Damascus, so that if he found any who belonged to the Way, men or women, he might bring them bound to Jerusalem. [3] Now as he was going along and approaching Damascus, suddenly a light from heaven flashed around him. [4] He fell to the ground and heard a voice saying to him, 'Saul, Saul, why do you persecute me?' [5] He asked, 'Who are you, Lord?' The reply came, 'I am Jesus, whom you are persecuting. [6] But get up and enter the city, and you will be told what you are to do.' [7] The men who were traveling with him stood speechless because they heard the voice but saw no one. [8] Saul got up from the ground, and though his eyes were open, he could see nothing; so they led him by the hand and brought him into Damascus. [9] For three days he was without sight, and neither ate nor drank.

A literalistic reading would claim, as Saul himself did on subsequent occasions, that he was on the receiving end of a divine revelation. He was riding along on the road to Damascus when a light from outside blinded him and a voice commanded him to cease his persecution of the followers of Jesus. We read in the subsequent verses that a follower of Jesus named Ananias comes to him and ministers to him, restoring his sight, and Saul, now to be called Paul, became a Christian apostle. There is no doubt that something happened to Saul of Tarsus that turned him into the formative genius behind the early theological understanding of Jesus. We can accept all that, we can even accept the apparently miraculous blindness that afflicted him, but we approach the event from within a different interpretative framework. Saul's passionate vehemence against the followers of Jesus would suggest that his attention had already been arrested by the movement he was persecuting. The blindness was psychogenic, a somatic expression of the turmoil in his soul, as he refused to acknowledge, refused to *see*, what his own heart was telling him: that Jesus of Nazareth had captured him for himself and would, if surrendered to, take over his entire life. The story of Paul's conversion can be accounted for without recourse to supernatural agency; it was a struggle that was resolved within his own heart. That change was the real miracle we call the resurrection and Paul's account is the closest we can get to the originating event. Later writers, the more restrained of whom got into the official New Testament, set out to satisfy human curiosity with more detailed descriptions of the event. One, called the Gospel of Peter, actually describes the stone rolling away by itself and three men emerging from the tomb, two of them helping the other, and the cross following.[3]

These attempts to describe the event of the resurrection are, for their day, not unlike the attempts by scientists to picture the moment before the Big Bang. They are attempts at explaining the event that is hidden from them by reading backwards from the reality that is before them.

This retrospective way of doing theology is fairly clear in the gospels. The resurrection was the time when the penny finally dropped for the disciples and they discovered who Jesus was. Though the gospels appear to follow a chronological sequence, they are packed with coded as well as overt claims about the significance of Jesus from the very beginning. In Mark's narrative, he signals the identity of Jesus at his baptism; Matthew and Luke from his birth; and John goes back to eternity in his prologue. We have to ask ourselves today, therefore: if that is how they expressed the significance of Jesus for them in their words, how might we do it today in ours?

I have found an approach proposed by John Bowker to be very helpful. It was difficult to get my head round it at first but, when I did, I saw that it had real power of application in many situations. It comes from the seventh century in a dispute between Jains and Buddhists. In these traditions, there is an ultimate truth called nirvana that is essentially one, even though it may be referred to by various names. This led Haribhadra, a Jain, to what has been called 'the logic of nirvana' and it goes like this:

If nirvana turns out to be nirvana, it is nirvana that nirvana turns out to be, even though you and I may have been thinking about it in approximate and opposing ways. If the Earth turns out to be spherical, it is spherical that the Earth turns out to be, even though you hold that it is round and I hold that it is flat. We are both wrong, but at least we are approximately wrong about something. We may argue, as Haribhadra did, and try to convince each other; and, in the end, one position may be more approximately right than the other. But it will still be about a spherical Earth that flat Earthers and round Earthers happen to be arguing. On the basis of this 'logic of Nirvana', Haribhadra concluded that 'It is impossible for thoughtful people to quarrel over the way in which one expresses one's loyalty to this truth. It follows also, in his view, that anyone who points the way (however approximately) to what is truly the case must be honoured . . .'[4]

In other words, thoughtful people should not quarrel over the different ways in which they express their loyalty to truth, because, if they are being honest, their disagreements are at least about something and all genuine attempts to struggle for truth must be honoured. This sounds a bit like a different version of Kuhnian paradigm theory. Aristotle was not bad Newton, but a different approximation to an understanding of the reality that was in front of them both. Applying the logic of nirvana to the resurrection means that, whatever it is, it cannot be threatened or damaged by what we make of it. Whatever the originating event was and however we interpret it, all that we see is its consequence in the lives of those who encountered it. As I have already suggested, the resurrection is like the Big Bang, which scientists hypothesise as the originating event in the life of the universe; it is not available to us except by guesswork and theory. Just as scientists engage in retrospective interpretation, by reading the effect that is the universe back to the unimaginable moment of its beginning, so theologians have read back from the effects on the disciples to a hypothesis as to what caused them. We could say, therefore, that there are two resurrections, but only one is available to us. The first is the originating event, the mythic resurrection, the big bang that ignited the Christian movement; the second is the effectual resurrection, which is the continuing impact of Jesus upon history. The interesting thing about the resurrection is not what was claimed, but who made the claim. The people who had deserted Jesus in fear and fled from his dying, somewhere found the courage to proclaim the meaning of his life; and that transformation, that turnaround, is what we mean by resurrection. I would say that the resurrection of Jesus is best understood, best used, as a symbol or sign of the human possibility of transformation. And that transformation can be experienced at both the personal and the social level; and one can lead to another.

I could suggest many examples of the transformative resurrection at work, including the long struggle against Apartheid in South Africa. But the example I want to offer is from the Civil Rights movement in the US, because in its origins it is a fascinating combination of personal change leading to social and political action. The campaign to give Afro Americans full civil and human rights began as an act of personal transformation in the black community itself. It all began when one tired black woman called Rosa Parks in Montgomery, Alabama, refused to go to the back of the bus. She was sitting on the front seat of the black section and was asked to give that seat up to a white man who got on at a later stop. She refused, a policeman was called and she was arrested. The day after Rosa Parks' arrest, Martin Luther King called a meeting. A leaflet was sent out to 50,000 black people. It said: 'Don't ride the bus to work, to town, to school, or any place Monday, December 5. A negro woman has been arrested and put in jail because she refused to give up her bus seat. Come to a mass meeting Monday at 7pm at the Holt Street Baptist Church for further instructions.'[5] This was the beginning of the famous bus boycott that changed American history. It was as simple as that. They knew they would have to pay for their refusal to submit any longer to their own daily humiliation; they knew they would have to face hatred and persecution; but something dropped away from them, some burden of fear or timidity or resignation. In resurrection language, a whole people walked out of the tomb of segregation because a woman had the courage to refuse to go to the back of the bus. That was a resurrection moment.

Resurrection is the refusal to be imprisoned any longer by history and its long hatreds; it is the determination to take the first step out of the tomb. It may be a personal circumstance that immobilises us, or a social evil that confronts us: whatever it is, we simply refuse any longer to accept it, because the logic of resurrection calls us to action. It follows, therefore, that if we say we believe in the resurrection it only has meaning if we are people who believe in the possibility of transformed lives, transformed attitudes and transformed societies. The action is the proof of the belief. So I end with what may appear to be a paradox: I can say I believe in *that* resurrection *then*, the Jesus resurrection, because I see resurrections now, see stones rolled away and new possibilities rising from old attitudes. If a belief is an action indicator rather than a purely mental event, belief in resurrection means that I must commit myself to the possibility of transformation. That means continuing to struggle with the intractability of my own nature; more importantly, it means joining with others in action to bring new life to human communities that are still held in the grip of death.

CHAPTER TEN

Putting it All Together

One year at midnight mass on Christmas Eve I began my sermon by reporting that an ancient manuscript had recently been discovered, dated by scholars to 70 CE. I pointed out that, while they disagreed about its authenticity, all thought that it was a remarkable and interesting document. It appeared to be an autobiographical meditation, written by Jonathan the son of Simon, inn keeper at Bethlehem at the beginning of the first century. A North American scholar called Professor Capote, I went on, had made a translation of the document and, instead of a sermon, I intended to read his version of the document. It started like this: 'I, Jonathan son of Simon, of Bethlehem in Judaea, wish to set down my memory of events that are now being spoken of and written about, most recently in a text called, *The Good News according to Luke*, which has recently come to my attention.' The sermon I preached that night was published in a British newspaper a few days later. Soon I was getting letters from people, asking how they could acquire copies of this ancient document. There was no ancient document. I was following an old religious tradition, by making up a story in order to put over a message. I had even planted a clue about what I was doing in the text of my sermon. I gave the name *Capote* to the scholar who had translated the document because Truman Capote, author of *Breakfast at Tiffany's*, had pioneered modern versions of this ancient technique in his book, *In Cold Blood*, about a multiple murder in a Kansas farmhouse. That book was neither fiction nor pure documentary, so the critics dubbed it *faction*. Capote used the form of fictional narrative, including imaginative reconstructions of lengthy, unrecorded conversations, to get inside the complexity of a hideous event. In a modest way, my Christmas sermon had been a similar exercise.

The Hebrew word for this technique is *midrash*, from a verb meaning to search out, to seek, to enquire. All religious traditions develop a literature of imaginative responses to their sacred writings. C.S. Lewis' *The Screwtape Letters* is a good example. This book, one of the most famous that Lewis wrote, purports to be letters from a junior demon to his supervisor, about his work of tempting a hapless human. A person who was unaware of such literary conventions might believe that the letters were authentic; and it is possible that Lewis got letters from some of his readers, asking for copies of the originals. An even more interesting exercise would be to imagine the situation after an overwhelming natural disaster, such as the impact of a massive meteorite that wipes out civilisation on earth, leaving few humans alive to rebuild society. A handful of fragments of the world's literature is later found in the ruins of an Irish monastery. If we imagine that among those remnants there were significant sections of the Book of Revelation from the New Testament, bits of Mark's gospel and large chunks of *The Screwtape Letters*, we would have enough to start scholars on a reconstruction of the beliefs of the group that lay behind the discovered fragments. It is intriguing to imagine what such a reconstruction of Christian beliefs in the twenty-first century would look like.

There is a lot of imaginative construction of this sort

in the New Testament, as there is in all ancient literature. Herodotus was not being dishonest when he put long speeches of his own construction into the mouths of generals in *The Persian Wars*; he was following the conventions of his craft. If we want to understand scripture, we have to read it within the literary conventions of its day. Theological development is obvious from even a cursory reading of the New Testament. Even the most untutored reader is able to detect considerable evolution in the interpretation of Jesus between Mark, almost certainly the first gospel to be written, and John, almost certainly the last. For example, many scholars believe that the whole of John is *midrash*, an imaginative theological construction that is the fruit of years of meditating on the meaning of Jesus. The majestic opening verses of the book are not an eye-witness account of eternity, but a meditation on how the spirit that energised the whole of creation from the beginning became human in Jesus. And the long discourses in that book can be understood not as verbatim recordings of monologues by Jesus, but as complex theological interpretations of his meaning for the young Christian movement. In the other three gospels, called the *synoptics* because they take a broadly similar view of Jesus, change and development are clearly traceable. We encounter difficulties in our use of the New Testament only if we bring to its study a forensic approach, in which the historic test becomes the main guide to its moral authenticity.

There is another characteristic of the New Testament which is just as important. This is what one scholar has called 'the backward development of New Testament Christology'.[1] The disciples of Jesus only gradually realised who he was and it was not until his death and resurrection that their understanding was complete: in this man God was encountered so intimately that the only way to describe the experience was to say that what God was, Jesus was. That high point of theological development came after the death of Jesus. When the gospels came to be written, however, the evangelists read that mature understanding of Jesus back into the narratives they created about him. Kierkegaard said we live life forward and understand it backward. We could apply that to the development of the Church's theological understanding of Jesus: the disciples lived their encounter with Jesus forward, but they read their completed understanding of his nature back into the stories they later told about him. So what we get in these narratives is retrospective theology, not recorded history. This means that we waste ourselves in fruitless debates about whether the accounts of the birth of Jesus are or could be historically accurate, about whether there was an actual massacre of the innocents and a flight of the holy family into Egypt, instead of trying to derive usable meaning for ourselves from these highly symbolic narratives, which are found only in Matthew's gospel. Matthew's gospel was probably written some years after the destruction of the Jewish Temple in 70 CE. The Christian movement began its life as a sort of Trotskyite tendency within Judaism, which tolerated a fair amount of diversity. The destruction of the Temple and its ancient tradition of sacrifice and ritual was a devastating blow to this ancient way of life. In time Judaism adapted to the crisis by replacing the priestly cult of animal sacrifice that had been based on the Temple with a rabbinical form of its tradition based on the synagogue. During this period of traumatic adjustment the status of the Christian sect must have been a topic of intense and painful disagreement, and there are ugly echoes of the controversy in John's gospel with its frequent and scornful reference to 'the Jews' because of their rejection of messianic claims made on behalf of Jesus by his followers in the synagogue communities. Matthew may have been writing for a beleaguered Christian community which was tempted to abandon its commitment to Jesus as Messiah, so he sets out to show that Jesus replaced Judaism and the Temple. One of the ways he does this is by loading his infancy narratives with highly symbolic events that portray Jesus as the successor to some of the great figures in Israel's past. The mysterious gentiles from the east, bearing their gifts of gold, incense and myrrh, establish Jesus as the successor to the three great symbolic figures of Jewish history, king, priest and prophet, gold representing kingship, incense priesthood and myrrh prophecy. By this powerfully coded narrative, Matthew sets Jesus at the centre of Jewish history as its fulfilment or culmination. Just as the Israelites were the victims of a wicked king who massacred Jewish babies, so was Jesus the target of a similar purge by Herod; and just as they were led out of slavery in Egypt by Moses, so Jesus returns from Egypt after Herod's death to fulfil his destiny as the redeemer of Israel.

[2:1] In the time of King Herod, after Jesus was born in Bethlehem of Judea, wise men from the East came to Jerusalem, [2] asking, 'Where is the child who has been born king of the Jews? For we observed his star at its rising, and have come to pay him homage.' [3] When King Herod heard this, he was frightened, and all Jerusalem with him; [4] and calling together all the chief priests and scribes of the people, he inquired of them where the Messiah was to be born. [5] They told him, 'In Bethlehem of Judea; for so it has been written by the prophet:

[6]"And you, Bethlehem, in the land of Judah,

    are by no means least among the rulers of Judah;
  for from you shall come a ruler
    who is to shepherd my people Israel."'

[7] Then Herod secretly called for the wise men and learned from them the exact time when the star had appeared. [8] Then he sent them to Bethlehem, saying, 'Go and search diligently for the child; and when you have found him, bring me word so that I may also go and pay him homage.' [9] When they had heard the king, they set out; and there, ahead of them, went the star that they had seen at its rising, until it stopped over the place where the child was. [10] When they saw that the star had stopped, they were overwhelmed with joy. [11] On entering the house, they saw the child with Mary his mother; and they knelt down and paid him homage. Then, opening their treasure chests, they offered him gifts of gold, frankincense, and myrrh. [12] And having been warned in a dream not to return to Herod, they left for their own country by another road.

[13] Now after they had left, an angel of the Lord appeared to Joseph in a dream and said, 'Get up, take the child and his mother, and flee to Egypt, and remain there until I tell you; for Herod is about to search for the child, to destroy him.'

[16] When Herod saw that he had been tricked by the wise men, he was infuriated, and he sent and killed all the children in and around Bethlehem who were two years old or under, according to the time that he had learned from the wise men.

[19] When Herod died, an angel of the Lord suddenly appeared in a dream to Joseph in Egypt and said, [20] 'Get up, take the child and his mother, and go to the land of Israel, for those who were seeking the child's life are dead.' [21] Then Joseph got up, took the child and his mother, and went to the land of Israel.[2]

This potent use of symbolic parallels to the history of

Israel is continued throughout the gospel, which includes a sojourn in the wilderness of forty days, paralleling the forty years in the wilderness after the exodus from Egypt; and the giving of a new law, in which the Sermon on the Mount replaces, for Christians, the giving of the Law on Mount Sinai. Matthew is trying to persuade his audience that the crisis they face points to Jesus as the fulfilment of traditional Judaism. This kind of polemical advocacy of Jesus as the successor of the old Judaism is promoted throughout the New Testament; it is the theme, for instance, of the highly symbolic Letter to the Hebrews. Dogmatic Christianity is the fruit of centuries of interpretation of the meaning of Jesus, and we see one stage of the process in this epistle. It is a brilliant attempt at a sustained metaphor to express the significance of Jesus for his earliest followers. Good preachers will recognise the genre because they spend their lives trying to find different ways of talking about Jesus that will fix him in the contexts of their hearers. Just as the prologue to John's gospel uses the Greek philosophical concept of *logos*, meaning the reason or animating principle that activates creation, to express the meaning of Jesus, so the author of Hebrews uses a symbolic system that would be very familiar to Jews.

Judaism has always engaged in heated debate within itself about the nature of its symbolic systems, those human constructs that are created to connect the human with the divine. Its most potent symbol at the time of Jesus was the Temple at Jerusalem, where the round of sacrifices and offerings connected its adherents with the mystery of God's demanding holiness. The Temple system of sacrifice was constantly challenged from within Judaism as an inappropriate way to express the human encounter with God. The prophets of the Hebrew Scriptures had condemned the sacrificial system that lay at the centre of the Temple cult because it had become an easy substitute for what God really wanted from the children of Israel, the sacrifices of mercy and justice for the poor. This ancient debate must have intensified after the physical destruction of the Temple. The author of the Letter to the Hebrews entered the debate, and offered his interpretation of Jesus as a new and better way of mediation between God and humanity than the Temple cult. Jesus replaced the Temple for Christians; just as Rabbinic or synagogue-based Judaism would replace it for Jews.

[9:1] Now even the first covenant had regulations for worship and an earthly sanctuary. [2] For a tent was constructed, the first one, in which were the lampstand, the table, and the bread of the Presence; this is called the Holy Place. [3] Behind the second curtain was a tent called the Holy of Holies. [4] In it stood the golden altar of incense and the ark of the covenant overlaid on all sides with gold, in which there were a golden urn holding the manna, and Aaron's rod that budded, and the tablets of the covenant; [5] above it were the cherubim of glory overshadowing the mercy seat. Of these things we cannot speak now in detail.

[6] Such preparations having been made, the priests go continually into the first tent to carry out their ritual duties; [7] but only the high priest goes into the second, and he but once a year, and not without taking the blood that he offers for himself and for the sins committed unintentionally by the people. [8] By this the Holy Spirit indicates that the way into the sanctuary has not yet been disclosed as long as the first tent is still standing. [9] This is a symbol of the present time, during which gifts and sacrifices are offered that cannot perfect the conscience of the worshiper, [10] but deal only with food and drink

and various baptisms, regulations for the body imposed until the time comes to set things right.

[11] But when Christ came as a high priest of the good things that have come, then through the greater and perfect tent (not made with hands, that is, not of this creation), [12] he entered once for all into the Holy Place, not with the blood of goats and calves, but with his own blood, thus obtaining eternal redemption. [13] For if the blood of goats and bulls, with the sprinkling of the ashes of a heifer, sanctifies those who have been defiled so that their flesh is purified, [14] how much more will the blood of Christ, who through the eternal Spirit offered himself without blemish to God, purify our conscience from dead works to worship the living God!

[15] For this reason he is the mediator of a new covenant, so that those who are called may receive the promised eternal inheritance, because a death has occurred that redeems them from the transgressions under the first covenant.[3]

It is difficult to understand the New Testament if we do not interpret it against the background of its defensive dispute with Judaism. One way of interpreting the story of the first Christian Pentecost in the Acts of the Apostles is to see it as coming from this same kind of literature of advocacy. Acts chapter 2 is an extended exercise in theological code, and we only get the message if we know the background, just as my Christmas sermon only made sense to people who were already familiar with the Gospel of Luke. We have already seen that one of the favourite techniques used by the New Testament writers is to take significant events from the Old Testament and repeat or echo them in a different context to show that Jesus had assumed the role that was previously filled by the great figures of the Hebrew Scriptures, such as Moses. The second chapter of the Acts of the Apostles provides us with another example of the way the New Testament echoes and develops themes from the Old Testament.

> [2:1] When the day of Pentecost had come, they were all together in one place. [2] And suddenly from heaven there came a sound like the rush of a violent wind, and it filled the entire house where they were sitting. [3] Divided tongues, as of fire, appeared among them, and a tongue rested on each of them. [4] All of them were filled with the Holy Spirit and began to speak in other languages, as the Spirit gave them ability.

The foundational event in the formation of Judaism was the exodus from Egypt. Borrowing the language of this pivotal event, the early Christians described the resurrection of Jesus as his exodus from the bondage of death. Fifty days after the exodus from Egypt the children of Israel arrived at Mount Sinai, where, in the midst of thunder and lightning, God made a contract with Israel, establishing them as his own people. According to one ancient Jewish writer, angels took the news of the bargain struck between Moses and God on Mount Sinai and carried it on tongues to the people of Israel camped out on the plain below.[4] In the same way, fifty days after Easter, the Christian exodus, something like the same process, is repeated at the feast of Pentecost, the Christian equivalent of the covenant on Mount Sinai, when the followers of Jesus are established as the nucleus of a new people of God, commissioned to take the good news of Jesus to the whole world. Another way of reading the Pentecost narrative is to see it as a Christian answer to the myth of the Tower at Babel, where God divided the human race into different languages to prevent it from building a scaffold up to heaven. At Pentecost the

[151]

division and confusion of humanity is reversed into a new unity in the spirit. The important thing to understand about this complex narrative is that it is making a simple claim: since that first Christian Pentecost, it has been through the Church that the meaning and message of Jesus, who is the fulfilment of Judaism, has been carried into the world.

Whatever side we want to take on the dispute that resulted in the separation of Christianity from its roots and led it to proclaim itself as the fulfilment or replacement of Judaism, we have to ask ourselves whether it has any point for us today, whether there is anything that we can use here in our search for a workable religious tradition. We ought to begin by admitting that there has always been considerable effrontery in the claim that Judaism has been superseded by Christianity. It can hardly be any surprise that it poisoned relations between Judaism and the Church for centuries. We ought to go on and admit that anti-semitism clearly has its roots here, though it culminated in the Holocaust in our own era. And we probably ought to accept that the dispute had its origins in a religious world-view that is of little use to us today, unless it is heavily re-interpreted.

I have already mentioned an aspect of religion called *apocalyptic*, and it is a theme I shall return to later in this book. One crucial aspect of *apocalyptic* was its focus on messianic expectation, on the arrival in history of God's anointed agent or *Christ* to inaugurate a reign of righteousness on earth. It is clear that the dispute between Christians and Jews in the first century focused on the claim that Jesus was the messiah or Christ. The early followers of Jesus clearly expected their faith in Jesus as messiah to be vindicated soon by his actual return in glory. Indeed, one of the main sources of strain and incoherence in Christianity has its origin in the contradiction between its pragmatic adaptation to the fact that Jesus did not return, so that Christianity had to settle down to the long haul of history, and its failure to jettison the strand in the Christian scriptures that confidently predicted his imminent return. The apocalyptic strand in Christianity has been a hunting ground for cranks in every generation, and its constant power to distort human judgement was clearly demonstrated at the end of the twentieth century by outbreaks of millenarian fantasy. The most elaborate apocalyptic in the New Testament is found in the last book of the Bible, the Book of Revelation. It is no accident that many of the people who become afflicted with religious psychosis betray a fatal knowledge of this strange and unpleasant document. It is from Revelation that movie directors and pulp novelists have picked up the famous symbol of the Triple Six, 666, the Mark of the Beast. And it is in Revelation that we read of the Battle of Armageddon, the final conflict between Good and Evil that was to take place at Megiddo, not far from Jerusalem. But the most fateful of the contributions of the Book of Revelation to religious madness of the sort that we saw at the end of the last century is the notion of the millennium itself:

> And I saw an angel come down from heaven, having the key of the bottomless pit and a great chain in his hand. And he laid hold on the dragon, that old serpent, which is the Devil, and Satan, and bound him a thousand years. And cast him into the bottomless pit, and shut him up, and set a seal upon him, that he should deceive no more, till the thousand years should be fulfilled: and after that he must be loosed a little season.[5]

The real battle for Christians today is not Armageddon, it

is the battle for a sensible approach to that ancient library of books we call the Bible. The Bible was written by human beings, with all the longings, prejudices and illusions that characterise us as a species. It is not an apocalyptic almanac, a mystical code book, an inerrant textbook for living. It is a compendium of a particular people's struggle with meaning; so it should encourage us to do the same in our day. Jesus will not return on the clouds to inaugurate a reign of righteousness on earth. The messianic hope, whether Jewish or Christian, understood as historic prediction or expectation, has clearly and repeatedly been falsified. We know, of course, that religious illusions are capable of absorbing all facts, even facts that falsify their claims, but those of us who want a religious tradition that has been purged of disabling fantasies ought to admit that the apocalyptic strand in Christianity can now be used only as a metaphor or symbol for the unquenchable human longing for a better society. In the same way, we ought to admit that the specific issue at dispute between Judaism and Christianity no longer makes much sense. Since we no longer expect the supernatural intrusion of a divine figure into human history to mend its hurt, whether it be the Jewish or the Christian messiah, we ought to close the books on a dispute that is based on a world-view that no longer makes sense to us. I would go further and suggest that liberal Jews and liberal Christians have more in common with each other than either group has with their own ultra-orthodox colleagues, who continue to hold the old tradition in the strictly traditional way.

This quarrel over the messianic status of Jesus within first-century Judaism had profound effects on Christianity and prompted it towards a fateful turning point that switched the emphasis from following the way *of* Jesus to believing things *about* Jesus. Gradually a Christian came to be thought of not as one who lives and acts in a certain way, but as one who holds certain convictions or theories. The trouble with religious convictions or beliefs is that, since we can rarely prove or disprove them, we get anxious about them and start quarrelling with people whose convictions or theories differ from our own. That is why Christianity has been riven with disputes from its earliest years, and it is probably one of the reasons why people in Europe are leaving it in droves today. One of the battlegrounds in Christian theology in our time is over *Orthodoxy*, from the Greek term for Right Opinion, Right Belief. The refinements that are offered by the different groups of disputing believers are endless, as the following example illustrates. The Christian doctrine of the atonement claims that the death of Jesus benefited the whole human race. There are several helpful ways of interpreting that claim, as well as some that are not. Conservative evangelicals believe in what is called the *substitutionary* atonement, which holds that God was so angry with humanity over our sinfulness that he demanded our punishment; Jesus, the sinless son of God, was substituted for us, took our punishment, literally dying in our place, and thereby appeased the anger of God. Sound evangelicals hold this precise refinement of an already rather complex set of ideas in their heads and they can be quite fierce in defending it. Because I did not hold the substitutionary theory of the atonement, I could never be invited to address the largest Christian student organisation at Edinburgh University, which requires sworn evidence of belief in this theory from its speakers. The trouble with theological disputes of this sort is that they have a self-fortifying effect on the protagonists who take pride in the particular characteristics of their belief system. The desire to belong to a gang, an exclusive community, particularly one that is blessed with knowledge that is hidden from others, is potently attractive to many, particularly the young. Christian theological history is filled with stories of groups who have developed theories of the election of themselves to salvation and the damnation of others; theories that demonstrate that their particular group has been exclusively endowed with divine truth, so that they possess a unique mission to the world and have a unique authority within it. Claims of this sort have been held and are still held by Christians.

It is the sheer unlikeliness of the truth of the claims that prompts people to scepticism and bewilderment as they contemplate them. We have already seen that centuries of falsification of the claims made about the precise date of the end of the world have had little effect on the protagonists of apocalypse, who simply go off and adjust their watches to the next timetable. As a doubter's response to this tendency to theological inflation, I would like to suggest that we ought to switch the emphasis in Christianity from belief to practice, from Ortho*doxy* to Ortho*praxis*, from believing things *about* Jesus to the imitation *of* Jesus. There would be three challenging elements in such a determination, none of them easy to follow. The first would be a resolution to love rather than condemn sinners; to seek to understand others rather than rush to judgement. The second element would be an active pity for the wretched of the earth that worked to change their lot. Finally, there would be a mistrust of power and violence, both personal and institutional, and an active opposition to them. This was the programme that got Jesus crucified. Following it today won't make us popular, but it would be a more creative response to the confusions of the human condition than the endless disputes over doctrine that have so disfigured Christian history.

CHAPTER ELEVEN

The Old Firm

John Donne said that truth stands on a huge hill, 'cragged and steep and he that will reach her, about must, and about must go'.[1] That is the approach I am adopting as I attempt to discover usable truth on the great mountain of wisdom and superstition that is the Christian tradition. In the last chapter I pointed to the paradox of theological development and how it read itself back into what appear to be chronological narratives of the life of Jesus, but are, in fact, highly coded documents. The other aspect of this which we have already noted, and one which is particularly awkward for us today, is the way narratives were created to echo or fulfil passages and traditions from the Hebrew Scripture. In the last chapter we considered the painful separation of the Christian movement from its matrix in Judaism and how that struggle coloured the language of the New Testament in a way that had fateful consequences for the Jewish people. Another side of this process was a systematic exercise in religious colonisation, whereby the Christian movement occupied the scriptures of the Hebrew tradition and assumed title to and ownership of them. Thereafter, as our bibles now attest, they were part of the 'old' testament, which was the forerunner to Christianity. God had created a 'new' testament or contract with a different Israel or special people, the Church, which was now heir to the promises and riches of Judaism. Stated as baldly as that, it appears to be a breathtakingly arrogant

[158]

exercise in theological imperialism; but we probably ought to acknowledge that it only appears monstrous because it was so successful. This kind of thing happens all the time, but the groups that go off from the parent body usually fade into insignificance. History is full of examples of sects who claimed to be the true inheritors of some tradition or other, but they usually end as footnotes in the story of the groups they repudiated. The study of schismatic groups is one of the interesting byways of human history. The effrontery of the Christian take-over of Judaism looks extraordinary today, only because the new movement became so powerful and turned with such ferocity upon its parent.

The truth I am looking for as I angle my way up the hill of Christian tradition is the meaning of Jesus for today, but to get there I have to make one more detour around the Christian Church. The Church is not, and never really has been, a single identifiable system, with one set of distinguishing characteristics, though it came closest to it in the West during the long ascendancy of Roman Catholicism. The classic way of talking about this is to point out that, speaking sociologically, church by definition means plurality and inclusiveness, whereas sect means singularity and exclusiveness. It is an inescapable fact that some people want only to belong to sects of the like-minded, however tiny. The perfect sect is probably a solitary individual with no one around to disturb his absolute sense that he alone is right. Most people recognise that there are many competing answers to the problems that obsess us and the issues that occupy us, so they instinctively organise themselves into larger wholes that allow diversity and the winnowing effect of controversy on their struggle with truth. We call these systems churches, from the Greek word for assembly. The church/sect distinction fits many institutions. You will sometimes hear politicians describe their party as 'a broad church' or 'big tent', because it represents a range of views, in contrast to the tiny political sects that occupy the edges of society. The church/sect typology is a useful place to start an exploration of the dynamics of the Christian Church.

At one time, I used to live opposite a living example of the sectarian mind. When I was a priest in Edinburgh in the 1970s, I lived a few yards from Princes Street in the city centre. At the foot of the Mound, next to the Royal Scottish Academy, there is a speakers' corner, and I used to spend a few minutes looking and listening during my Sunday afternoon walk, when most of the action took place. One of the regulars fascinated me. He was virulently anti-Catholic, and spent his time proving that the Pope was Anti-Christ. Like many soap-box orators, he was a brilliant debater. When handling hecklers he was quick with historic facts and illustrations, all proving how evil Rome was and how unbiblical its doctrines were. I used to wonder what kind of life he led, this man who was so clearly obsessed with the institution he hated. What did he do the rest of the week? Did he spend all his time studying pamphlets put out by those dismal Reformation protection societies, with their endless conspiracy theories; or did he lead an otherwise normal life in the bosom of a happy family? I got the answer years later, when he moved with a large dog into a basement in the crescent opposite. Several times a day I would pass him in the street with his dog, walking swiftly, head down. He lived alone, spoke to and was visited by no one. On my way to the Cathedral in the early morning I would pass his lonely figure. It was a triumph when I got him to return my good morning

greeting with a grunt, although there was never any
eye contact. Then, one day, he was gone. For me, he
encapsulated the imperative of the sect mentality, ending
up on his own, hidden away in an anonymous basement
flat, nursing God knows what fantasies about the dangers
that swarmed above his head.

The main characteristic of the sectarian mind is fear,
whether of some kind of pollution or of ultimate damnation. Most of us know that there are weird people out
there, but we are usually undisturbed by their monomania,
unless they manage to take over some institution that is
important to us, and drive it in their own direction. In
Yeats' phrase, 'the worst are full of passionate intensity',[2]
while the rest of us are enjoying our ordinary lives. Many
obsessive sectarians are probably also psychotic, but I do
not want to trespass into that area, except to point out
that at the root of much religious sectarianism is a kind of
ultimate fear. Religious anxiety goes back a very long way
and is probably behind the ancient sacrifice system, with
its detailed placation of angry gods. The sacrifice system
itself is almost extinct, though William Dalrymple found
remnants of it in Eastern Orthodoxy during his travels in
the Middle East when researching his book *From the Holy
Mount*. The language of placation, however, is very much a
part of the Christian tradition still. George Mackay Brown
gives us an entertaining example in his book *An Orkney
Tapestry*.

> 'We'd do weel to pray,' said a North Ronaldsay fisherman
> to his crew as another huge wave broke over them.
> It had been a fine day when they launched the boat.
> Then the sudden gale got up. Willag was a Kirk elder.
> The skipper told him to start praying. Spindrift lashed in
> and over.

'O Lord,' said Willag, 'Thou art just, Thou art wonderful, Thou art merciful, great are thy works, Thou
art mighty.'

Willag faltered in his litany of praise. The boat wallowed
through a huge trough.

'Butter him up,' cried the skipper, 'butter him up'.[3]

It is easy to figure out the connection between the exaggerated language of praise and worship in the Christian
liturgy and ancient styles of address of the sort that are
only now applied to the royal family in Britain. The
presence of sectarian anxiety has a less straightforward
background, but I would like to suggest one possible
explanation for its survival in Christianity. Behind much
of that anxiety there lies that ancient human response
to oppression I have already described as Apocalyptic.
The people of Israel existed on a narrow corridor of
land between opposing empires and they experienced
constant oppression in their turbulent history. The social
and economic system of biblical times was a domination
system that required for its maintenance not only a peasant
class poised permanently between poverty and destitution,
but an expendable class who lived in the margins and
shadows of society. Apocalyptic is the projection of the
hopes of beaten people onto the future. Surely a righteous
God will act soon to overthrow oppression and wrong
and establish a reign of justice on earth. This was one
of the themes present in Israel in the days of Jesus, and
its protagonists contributed an important strand to the
complex religious situation of the time. John the Baptist
almost certainly belonged to this tradition. His baptism
was an act of preparation for the great cleansing that was
to come, when the land would be purified with fire. It is less
easy to define the final position that Jesus took, though it is

clear that he went through an apocalyptic phase, a subject to which I shall return in a subsequent chapter.

A fascinating example of the same phenomenon can be found closer to our own time in the reaction of the American Indians to American imperialism. Here are the words of a scholar on the subject:

> The Indians suffered loss of independence, economic hardship, and the breakdown of their order of society, and they experienced nativistic revivals passively advocating continued belief in Indian culture by Indians, undertook militant wars of religion like that led by the Prophet and Tecumseh, believed in messianic movements emphasising high morality, like those in the Pacific Northwest, and even began proselytising among themselves as in the case of Indian Shakerism or the Peyote cult.[4]

The apocalyptic strain in religion induces in its adherents a sense of special election to the glories of the end time, as well as a conviction that disciplined holiness will help to bring the time nearer, hence the movements into the purifying wilderness that characterise the phenomenon. More fatefully, perhaps, is the fear of being lost or rejected at the end time, by colluding with the enemy or being corrupted by their values. The sectarian mind of today is captivated by the mysterious remnants of the apocalyptic tradition that are present in the scriptures of the Christian tradition. They have a tremendous sense of matters of eternal importance being acted out, which promise either eternal bliss or eternal torment. Getting it right, being among the elect, is vital. This probably accounts for the high anxiety that characterises these systems, their cruelty and dismissiveness. If you are fighting your way into the fall-out shelter to escape from the coming nuclear winter, you can't afford to be too magnanimous. I have placed most of the weight of apocalyptic anxiety upon sectarian Christians, but they have simply carried to an extreme an element that was in the consciousness of the Church from the beginning. As we have already seen, in its teaching about hellfire, the Church preached a message that might be described as delayed apocalyptic. High-level anxiety infected the Christian mind very early in its history, and its roots seem to lie in the apocalyptic hope of beaten people.

If the sectarian impulse has its roots in anxiety over being on the wrong side at the end of the world, then the impulse behind the formation of the inclusivity of church is the complexity of the human search for truth. Truth is rarely simple and seldom obvious, which is why mature institutions recognise the importance of conflict and disagreement. Christianity was born in conflict, and it has been characterised by conflict ever since. The Church's obsession with heresy is witness to this fact. Heresy is a bit of the truth, a part of a complicated whole that is exaggerated at the expense of other perspectives. But the heretical imperative is fundamental to the testing of truth and the widening of its scope. For centuries the Church has wrestled with the meaning of Jesus and continues to do so today. Jesus did not found the Church, nor appoint office bearers with clearly defined job descriptions, nor codify a set of official teachings. What he did was to place himself and God on the side of those the official system defined as expendable outcasts, among whom he generated an excitement about this new understanding of God. He did more than question the received order: he treated it as though it did not exist; he acted as if his own vision of the welcoming father were already a universal reality. He was executed by the system he stood against; he, too, was an expendable man, but the vision did not die with him. It lived on, mixed up with elements of the old system he had opposed, as well as with elements of apocalyptic longing and messianic hope.

His earliest followers disagreed among themselves about the meaning of the strands of apocalyptic expectation that had been present in his thinking. They disputed over whether they were to stay in Jerusalem, waiting for him to return and vindicate their faith in him as the messiah, or whether he was already mystically present with them through a message that was to be taken to the ends of the earth. The struggles around these issues are echoed in the pages of Paul's letters, and in the Acts of the Apostles. By the end of the first century the Christian movement had separated from Judaism, though it was still confused about the timetable for the great apocalyptic return, which was to become an unpredictable and volatile element in Christian history; and was poised to become a universal movement, a world-wide Church. But what did all of this have to do with Jesus? There is an obvious conflict between the spirit of Jesus and the dynamics of institutional power; so to be a follower of Jesus and a member of the Church, particularly if you are an official, creates a difficult tension. Let me try to explain that paradox.

The great Roman Catholic New Testament scholar, Raymond Brown, died unexpectedly a couple of years ago. In his scholarship, as in his style as a lecturer, he was an eirenic man of the centre in the various disputes that rage round the historical status of the New Testament and the emergence of the Christian Church. In a series of lectures he gave in London in 1998 on 'The Emergence of the Christian Church'[5] he spent a lecture meditating on

[165]

the paradox that any institution should have emerged to represent and maintain in history the memory, the words and the acts of Jesus of Nazareth. The Church has been called the extension of the incarnation and the phrase is worth a moment's thought. The theological short-hand for the developed understanding of the status of Jesus of Nazareth is that, while he was truly and actually a man, a human male in every sense, he was also the incarnation of God, the vessel chosen by God to enter history and 'become flesh', to use the language of John's gospel. It is the Church's role and vocation to continue that divine work, so it could be described as the extension of the incarnation through history. His earthly life having ended in his crucifixion, resurrection and ascension, or return to heaven, his presence is now continued or extended through the Christian Church.

In his lecture on Jesus, Brown meditated on the unlikely paradox that any institution could represent this man because institutions, by their very nature, have to follow particular laws if they are to survive and prosper; and the main law of institutional survival is that the many take precedence over the few. If institutions are to endure they have to place a higher value on their own endurance than on loyalty to individuals, no matter how attractive or charismatic they may be. The patron saint of all institutions is Caiaphas, the High Priest who determined the death of Jesus. The following incident from John's gospel is a perfect example of institutional pragmatism:

Then gathered the chief priests and the Pharisees a council, and said, What do we? for this man doeth many miracles. If we let him thus alone, all men will believe on him: and the Romans shall come and take away both our place and nation. And one of them, named Caiaphas, being the high priest that same year, said unto them, Ye know nothing at all. Nor consider that it is expedient for us, that one man should die for the people, and that the whole nation perish not.[6]

When the situation is as stark as that, most of us would probably make the same choice. The moral logic always points to the necessary sacrifice of one or two for the sake of the larger whole, in this case, according to unanswerable high priestly logic, the nation. Jesus was supremely uninterested in that logic. His whole attention seems to have been focused upon the individual sacrificed for the larger good, the person expended or sacrificed or declared redundant by the institution in question, whether religious or political. He would not have lasted long as a tutor in an agricultural college because he said that the good shepherd should leave the ninety-nine sheep in the wilderness and go in search of the one who was lost. And the local business organisation would certainly have refused him membership because, when asked how many times we should forgive the local embezzler, seven times perhaps?, he replied 'seventy times seven', which is an oriental way of saying 'always'.[7] This is an impossible way to run any institution and it has never really been tried except by a few saints and Zen masters, as the following story of a noted Japanese teacher illustrates:

When Bankei held his seclusion weeks of meditation, pupils from many parts of Japan came to attend. During one of these gatherings a pupil was caught stealing. The matter was reported to Bankei with the request that the culprit be expelled. Bankei ignored the request. Later the pupil was caught in a similar act and again Bankei

[167]

disregarded the matter. This angered the other pupils, who drew up a petition, asking for the dismissal of the thief, stating that otherwise they would leave in a body. When Bankei had read the petition he called everyone before him. 'You are wise brothers,' he told them, 'you know what is right and what is wrong. You may go somewhere else to study if you wish, but this poor brother does not even know right from wrong. Who will teach him if I do not? I am going to keep him here even if all the rest of you leave.' A torrent of tears cleansed the face of the brother who had stolen. All desire to steal had vanished.

That is the authentic voice of the saint, but you don't make saints chief executive officers, even in churches. You manage by the logic of expedience, the logic that preserves the institution first and regards the plight of the individual, if it regards it at all, last. Caiaphas, as the author of the fourth gospel recognised, 'prophesied' that Jesus had to die by the logic of nation and Temple, a logic that will always prevail in society because who can object to the calculus of the happiness of the greatest number over the misery of the single individual? Well, Jesus apparently did, hence the paradox of any institution representing him or extending his presence in history. The radical nature of the approach of Jesus came home to me with almost revelatory force when I read something that Hannah Arendt had said about her people, the Jews, and the fact that for centuries they had no place in the world. Speaking of the historic placelessness of the Jews, she said: 'the Jewish people are a classic example of a worldless people maintaining themselves throughout thousands of years . . . this worldlessness which the Jewish people suffered in being dispersed, and which – as with all people who are pariahs – generated a special warmth among those who

belonged, changed when the state of Israel was founded.'[8]
It is obvious that the State of Israel, founded in response
to years of persecution that tried to remove Jews from
the world, now follows the classic logic of expedience
in organising its own affairs, the logic of Caiaphas that
sacrifices others for its own safety, the ethic that governs
every nation. But something profound was lost when the
Jewish people, like the rest of us, found a place in the world
to inhabit. Hannah Arendt goes on: 'Yes, one pays dearly
for freedom. The specifically Jewish humanity signified
by their worldlessness was something very beautiful . . .
this standing outside all social connections, the complete
open-mindedness and absence of prejudice that I experienced, especially with my mother, who also exercised it
in relation to the whole Jewish community. Of course, a
great deal was lost with the passing of all that. One pays
for liberation.'[9]

I would like to suggest that this worldlessness or identification with the powerless is the key to the mystery of
Jesus. This radical identification with the outcast, those
without place or world in the organised scheme of things,
is expressed by Dominic Crossan in his version of the
beatitudes:

Only the destitute are innocent
Only those who have no bread have no fault
Only the wretched are guiltless
Only the despised are blameless[10]

Everyone who is successful in life is complicit in the way
the world works, the way of institutional power, the way
that creates expendable people who may be sacrificed for
the sake of the larger group. Occasionally, one who has

previously belonged to such a centre of power is sacrificed by it or thrown aside, and a stunned disbelief is the usual reaction to the event. To find that you have become No One is devastating for the victim, for whom old friends and colleagues suddenly turn into strangers. You get something of the flavour of this process from the movie *The Insider* with Al Pacino and Russell Crowe, which is based on a true story. The character played by Crowe is persuaded to blow the whistle on corrupt Big American Tobacco. He loses everything as a result, including his family and reputation. The brilliance of Crowe's understated performance is that, largely through subtle movements in his face and eyes, he suggests baffled helplessness at the way the organised world has suddenly turned against him, thrown him out and made him placeless and worldless, a man without significance.

In Jesus, we find one who placed himself alongside the expendable people of history and saw them as individuals with particular histories and uniqueness. That was why he was loved and surrounded by the people who had no place in the world; and it was why he was finally destroyed by the world. The term 'world' is interesting here. It is obvious that we are all, unlucky as well as lucky, living in the same world; but in the New Testament there is a use of the word that suggests another meaning than planet earth. The Gospel of John, in particular, has a strong sense of 'the world' as an organised structure of power and privilege that owes allegiance only to itself and even resists the approach of God: 'He was in the world, and the world came into being through him; yet the world did not know him. He came to what was his own, and his own people did not accept him.'[11] I shall come back to the implications of this understanding of Jesus as the one from outside who identifies himself with the worldless ones. Let me return now to Raymond Brown's wry acknowledgement that there is something odd about any organised system, any 'world', claiming to represent this man from the outside, this man without a place.

The paradox is that we have only heard of Jesus through an institution that has not experienced worldlessness for a very long time. This was the point Raymond Brown mused on in his lecture, but he did not offer any solution to the problem. The expendable man of Nazareth is now represented by an institution that follows the logic of all worldly institutions, the logic of expedience; yet we would not even know about the paradox if it weren't for the Church. There is something mysterious about this paradox, but it is part of the genius of power to co-opt and therefore to neutralise its opponents. That is why Alasdair McIntyre said that 'All power tends to co-opt and absolute power co-opts absolutely.'[12]

An example of this is provided by a fourth-century historian, a courtier bishop called Eusebius, who wrote a sycophantic life of the Emperor Constantine. Constantine believed that his victory in 312 at Rome's Milvian Bridge over his imperial rival Maxentius had been obtained by Christ's power. The night before the battle he had a dream in which he saw the symbol of the cross with the motto underneath, *in hoc signo vinces*: in this sign conquer. He had the sign turned into a banner under which he fought the following day. It worked. He won the battle and converted to Christianity. His subsequent policy was to bind the Church to his empire with the closest possible ties and use it as a unifying factor. Inevitably, he involved himself with the internal affairs of the Church, including debates over abstruse items of Christian doctrine. One of the most far-reaching of his interventions concerned the dispute over the true nature of Christ, whether he was fully God from all eternity, as well as fully man. To resolve the dispute, Constantine summoned the bishops to Nicea in 325 and ordered them to sort out their theological differences. When the Council reached a successful conclusion, Constantine invited the bishops to an imperial banquet. Here is how Eusebius, the first of a long line of episcopal creeps, gushingly describes it:

> Detachments of the bodyguard and troops surrounded the entrance of the palace with drawn swords, and through the midst of them the men of God proceeded without fear into the innermost of the Imperial apartments, in which some were the Emperor's companions at table, while others reclined on couches arranged on either side. One might have thought that a picture of Christ's kingdom was thus shadowed forth, and a dream rather than reality.[13]

Historians have traditionally seen this event as the final triumph of the Church and the beginning of its long dominance of European history. It established dogmatic Christianity in a long partnership with the world of political power that became known as Christendom, and only in our day is it in its final stages of dissolution. So glorious and powerful was the institution of Christendom that it was almost impossible to see through it to the man who stood behind it, the peasant from Galilee who had refused to cringe before the very power that crucified him and was later officially to deify him. The fascinating thing about our day is that, as the political and theological structures of Christendom crash down before our eyes, we can see once again, through the rubble and dust of the centuries, a clearer picture of the prophet of Nazareth.

The way scholars have described that evolution from the man of Nazareth to the God-Man of Nicea is to talk about the movement from the Jesus of History to the Christ of Faith. This is only one way of talking about theological development in early Christianity, and there are those who would repudiate the distinction that is implied in that particular form of words. Nevertheless, the advantage of using it is that it captures the historic nature of the movement from Nazareth to Nicea, from the flesh and blood Jesus to the heavenly Christ of the Catholic centuries. One thing is certainly true: from the beginning there has been development and change in the understanding of Jesus and his meaning within the Christian community. As with all theological disputes, there is no absolutely incontrovertible way of resolving the dispute about the true nature of Jesus, later called the Christ. This is where theological constructs or myths are unlike Kuhnian paradigms. I have already pointed out that science has followed an expanding path through the use of paradigms that work till they are replaced in a scientific revolution. Obviously, scientific paradigms are testable in a way that theological myths are not, but we can still make use of the Kuhnian insight as we struggle with its meaning and application to religion. And this is where I must show my own hand, by disclosing an operating principle that governs the approach I have taken in this book.

Since there is no way we can get in touch with the metaphysical or supernatural realm that is on the other side of the claims made about Jesus, I believe that we should now use these claims to define and characterise the way we live in this world and not as descriptions of another world beyond this one that we can have no direct knowledge of, including certain knowledge that it exists. What I want to offer as a programme of action is theological *pragmatism* as opposed to theological *positivism*. Theological positivism claims that, through revelation, we are given true and saving information about that reality we call the supernatural, or heaven, or the divine realm, or the other world. The 'truth' bit does not particularly bother me. If you tell me that you know that there is another heavenly reality beyond this one and that you know something about what goes on there, I hope I will have the grace to listen politely and not intrude upon convictions that are clearly important to you. If you tell me that unless I also hold the same views I cannot be 'saved' and that something awful and eternal will happen to me after death, I will be less inclined to listen graciously. Moreover, I will detect in your theology not just your private opinion about unknowable matters, but a kind of religious abuse, a power-play, that is clearly designed to pressurise me into re-arranging my mind so that it can accommodate the essential items you insist on installing there. To use Tillich's language, if you insist that the myth of the incarnation has to be understood in its literal or unbroken sense, then you are in danger of excluding me from its value altogether, because I am unable to submit to your particular version of it, which goes something like this: there is a god who is in some sense a discrete and definable being from whom we have been alienated by sin, original as well as actual, thereby creating a state of hostile separation between us. A long line of ambassadors from God, sent to make peace, have been systematically rejected and many of them killed. Finally God sends his only son to reconcile the world to himself. And he sends him to an unknown family in a nowhere town, where he is born of a woman without the sexual intervention of a human male. The salvation of the world depends upon its hearing about this event and coming to acknowledge the divine status of the child born in such remote anonymity.

Used as myth, metaphor or poetry, this beautiful story can be interpreted in several meaningful ways; taken literally, it is not just far-fetched, it is morally arbitrary. If God is able to pull off such an extraordinary miracle, and some others recorded as backup to the claim, why does he not exert his power in a more morally obvious way to alter the evil balance of power in the world? If God does choose to intervene and has the power to, why intervene in this way rather than in some more obvious way? I have been preaching long enough to know that highly sophisticated answers can be given to these queries, but all of them beg the question of the literalness of the myth, and thereby deprive it of its poetic power. No matter how subtle the new theological justifications of the myth are, they are inevitably confronted by the frankly and unavoidably mythological and pre-scientific language of the story. In a pre-quantum, flat-earth universe the literal details of the myth would be easier to accept because in the ancient world there was an acceptance of constant traffic between the divine and the human spheres.

Let me repeat myself: since I do not want to interfere in the devices people use to express their religious longings and convictions, I would not want to try to shift someone from a literalistic to a metaphorical understanding of the incarnation, or from the unbroken to the broken myth. My resistance to literalists is roused on two grounds. The first is when proponents of the unbroken myth say theirs is the only true way to hold it; secondly, and more importantly, I resist when I am told that holding the unbroken myth is not only 'true' but 'saving', that it must be held to avoid damnation. Humans do all sorts of things with language, with words, including the language of religion. I simply want to make space in Christianity for another way of using the traditional language. Let me now offer a sketch of what that use might be.

In recent years I have become fascinated by the theme of the hidden God and the unknown Christ. Encounters with the unknown Christ are surprisingly frequent in the New Testament. In the resurrection stories we have several accounts of Christ appearing to uncomprehending disciples, who think he is an interesting stranger, such as on the Road to Emmaus in the Gospel of Luke or on the shore of the Sea of Galilee in the Gospel of John. And there are occasions in the teaching of Jesus when the same point is made. The most dramatic version of this is found in the great parable of judgement in Matthew 25. At the end of history, people are separated into two groups, both of whom are surprised by the verdict that is delivered about them. On the one side are those who thought they were paid-up believers in Christ, who find themselves excluded because they have not served him. When they express their puzzlement at this perverse judgement, by reciting creeds and rehearsing their membership in various organisations for the defence of the faith, they are told that because they have not clothed the naked, fed the hungry, visited prisoners or given cold water to the thirsty, they are not on the side of Christ. But the surprise of the pious is as nothing compared with the surprise of those who are accepted. They have had little or no time for religion in their lives. They think it makes too many unverifiable claims and is responsible for too much hatred. They themselves don't really know what to believe, except that cruelty and indifference are curses upon the world. So they don't make many claims for themselves, but they volunteer a couple of times a month to feed the homeless, and some of them write to black prisoners on Death Row in the Christian State of Texas. They are as suspicious of politicians as they are of clergy, but they keep up the pressure on government to do something for the people who are not doing as well out of the economic system as they are. They don't much like the way the Church has turned the compassionate anger of the young prophet of Nazareth into dogma, but they admire the man himself and sometimes wonder if they haven't rubbed up against him at the odd demo against Third World Debt and the Arms Trade.

I used to try to place myself prudently on both sides of this judgement divide. I was theologically conservative and socially radical. I remember trying to get the slogan 'incense and drains' accepted as a motto for the Catholic Renewal movement because I thought both worship and decent housing were important for people. Theologically, I was pretty intense and now I think I know why. In the late 1960s I emerged from a period of radical doubt about the whole Christian doctrinal system, and I fell into a very common trap: I reacted against my own uncertainties by attacking doubt and uncertainty in others. A closet sceptic, I condemned in others what I was too afraid to look at in myself. My first book was an attack on the kind of theology I myself now write. All along, I can now see, I was my own enemy, the opponent of the other self within, the person who doubted that theological propositions actually represented metaphysical realities, actually described the situation in the heavenly realm. My anxieties about all of this caused me to engage in a classic projective identification and condemn in others what I secretly believed in my own heart. It is one of the deepest ironies of my life that I ended up in my sixties the kind of bishop that I attacked when I was a priest in my thirties. 'The whirligig of time brings in its revenges', as Mr Shakespeare well knew. As T.S. Eliot put it, I have ended up where I started, but now I think I know the place for the first time.

I am writing this because I think a liberating truth underlies it. I have come to believe passionately that we should treat a belief as 'a habit of action' rather than as an accurate representation of metaphysical reality, to quote Charles Sanders Peirce.[14] People who adopt a pragmatic approach to Christianity, because they are agnostic about the reality status of theological statements, ask themselves what action this or that belief commits them to, not whether it accurately represents the home life of God. And it brings us back to the parable of judgement in Matthew 25 and all those other stories of the unfound Christ, such as the story of the fourth wise man who did not make it to Bethlehem on time because he went to the aid of a poor widow. Each time he thought he was getting close to the Christ child, another unfortunate person would demand his assistance. Worn out with all his wandering and care of the suffering, he discovers that he has been in Bethlehem, worshipping the Christ child, all the time.

To demythologise the myth of the incarnation is not to dilute it, but to charge it with a profound and daunting ethical meaning. It calls us to a recognition that God is now to be found in the human, especially among the worldless, the disregarded ones, such as the Holy Family and the poor who welcomed them. To claim to believe in the incarnation is to commit ourselves to a radical commitment to the meaning of God not in verbal propositions, but in human lives, their joys and sorrows. If our talk does not serve this end, does not have a radical ethical imperative, then the Word that was made flesh in Jesus is simply made Word again in the Church. It is a chastening experience to realise that you have largely given your life to talking *about* Jesus, weaving words round the mystery of his meaning, rather than trying to walk in his footsteps. 'Poor little talkative Christianity' said E.M. Forster and, my God, he was right. And it is not just the boring talk, though there's been an ocean of that, it is the cruel talk, the judgement talk, the superior talk, the dismissive talk, the 'I have the truth and you don't' talk that is so crucifying. Crucifying, yes. I know it's a bit late to have made the discovery, but isn't it time we dismantled all the calvaries our words have built for Christ and simply tried to follow him, preferably in silence?

PART THREE

What is Left of Christianity

He comes to us as One unknown, without a name, as of old, by the lake-side, He came to those men who knew Him not.

Albert Schweitzer, *The Quest of the Historical Jesus*

CHAPTER TWELVE

The Outsider

The American composer Aaron Copland said somewhere that we are in need of a usable past. It helps us to negotiate our own journey if we have maps from the past to guide us. These maps are the traditions of our forebears, their reflections on how they made their own journey and understood its meaning. Education, formally understood, is the way we pass on the tradition. Societies which have achieved stability and duration usually do this best, in the sense of handing on a coherent guidance package for the journey of life. The beauty of such societies is that they inculcate the acceptance of a common view of things, a group narrative that both interprets and directs every aspect of the journey. Nietzsche has many illuminating things to say about this process: 'History teaches that the best-preserved tribe among a people is the one in which most men have a living communal sense as a consequence of sharing their customary and indisputable principles – in other words, in consequence of a common faith. Here the good, robust mores thrive; here the subordination of the individual is learned and the character receives firmness, first as a gift and then is further cultivated.'[1] He then goes on to offer one of his most brilliant insights:

The danger to these strong communities founded on homogeneous individuals who have character is growing stupidity, which is gradually increased by heredity, and which, in any case, follows all stability like a shadow. It is the individuals who have fewer ties and are much more uncertain and morally weaker upon whom spiritual progress depends in such communities; they are the men who make new and manifold experiments. Innumerable men of this sort perish because of their weakness without any very visible effect; but in general, especially if they have descendants, they loosen up and from time to time inflict a wound on the stable element of a community. Precisely in this wounded and weakened spot the whole structure is inoculated, as it were, with something new; but its over-all strength must be sufficient to accept this new element into its blood and assimilate it. Those who degenerate are of the highest importance wherever progress is to take place; every great progress must be preceded by a partial weakening. The strongest natures hold fast to the type; the weaker ones help to develop it further.[2]

It is important to understand the use of the terms *degenerate* and *morally weak* in that quotation. There is always a strong undercurrent of irony in what Nietzsche writes, so we probably ought to understand the meaning of the terms from the point of view of the strong guardians of the tradition in question. In Nietzschean language, the strongest natures will have interiorised the tradition most completely and will practise it unselfconsciously. From their point of view, any questioning of the tradition and any weakness in fulfilling it will be defined as degeneracy and corruption. We have all encountered exemplars of powerful traditions, of both the strong and stupid types. There is the strong conservative male, perhaps a high-ranking officer in a uniformed profession, who has completely internalised the tradition that bred him and repeatedly risked his life in its defence. These descendants of the warrior class have usually had to eschew political involvement, but they are inescapably bound in to the conservation of the tradition whose customs forbid them to be transparently political. They are, in fact, a highly politicised class, though usually in a profoundly conservative sense. They would die for the protection of the system that has produced them and of which they are the highest type. People who find themselves in these guardian roles often have a high practical intelligence, but they are rarely reflective or open to doubt; there may even be a strong genetic predisposition in them to the unquestioning acceptance of system and order. They are often intolerant of radical reformers, whom they usually dismiss with colourful contempt. Further down the chain of authority from these strong types we find the truly stupid members of traditional communities. They are usually rather shallow beneficiaries of the prevailing system who have done little to protect or extend it, but they offer it the homage of their uncomprehending benediction.

One of the many paradoxes of human development is illuminated here. The duration of a tradition is important to societies that prize stability and continuity, but the price they pay is a level of stagnation and stupidity that can end by threatening the safety of the tradition itself because they inhibit its evolution and development. The strong types end up as fundamentalists who can only 'defend tradition in the traditional way', to repeat a formula I have already used, and thereby put it at risk. Nietzsche's insight here is that it is precisely those who deviate from the tradition, because of their proneness to doubt and reflection, who provide the means for its development and continuance. The very people who are persecuted by the system for their heresy and corruption may be the agents that preserve whatever is enduringly sound in the tradition in question.

A deeper version of the same paradox is that the founders who become the passionate focus of fundamentalist loyalty in a later era were originally heretics in their native context, corrupters of the traditions that nurtured them. This would appear to suggest that a tradition must be continuously subverted and re-invented if it is to have enduring life; and it is the wounding that this process inflicts that inoculates the body with the new element that helps it to develop further.

One of the most important elements in the evolution of human institutions is the emergence of the difficult customer within the system itself, the radical who starts to question its very being, the reformer who calls for changes in the way it runs. We could develop a whole theory of education from that quotation from Nietzsche. A fundamental part of the education of the young has to be their enculturation into the tradition of the community to which they belong. This is the conservative imperative and it is probably best done by traditional disciplines. The idea is to instil in young people the best of the culture to which they belong. This is obviously a more complex task in multicultural than in monocultural societies, but the educational methods need not be so different. It will be an essentially conservative process that imparts the tradition to the emerging generation, by handing on to it the knowledge that has been accumulated by the best minds and institutions of the community. The second part of the process will be the deconstruction of the tradition that has been previously internalised. We cannot move a tradition on if we have not mastered it, which is why great innovators and revolutionaries have always profoundly absorbed the tradition that they later played such an important part in transforming. According to the philosopher Richard Rorty, a complete education will involve both of these very different processes, one essentially conservative, the other essentially radical.[3] Schools should be conservative institutions, intent on imparting the tradition that has developed so far; universities should be radical institutions, intent on interrogating the tradition and moving it on further. Liberals often fail to make this distinction in their theory of education and try, too quickly, to bring young people to the questioning of traditions they have not yet understood. We need subversives who have mastered the tradition so thoroughly that they know instinctively that it must be constantly undermined if it is to have any hope of enduring. Because they have taken its values so deeply into themselves, they understand that it must be constantly challenged if it is not to become lazy and oppressive. Jesus seems to have been this kind of creative subversive. He understood and observed the code of his people, but he knew that it had to be challenged if it was to continue to serve humanity and not the other way round. We are faced in Christianity today with a similar imperative of subversion, but in order to adapt the tradition that has grown round Jesus, we must first try to understand it.

All we have to go on are the texts of the New Testament and some other writings that did not make it into that official Church publication. As I have already tried to make clear, the texts themselves have been a constant battleground and nothing that is incontrovertible can be said about them. Speaking personally, I have occupied most of the notches on the continuum of interpretation, except the fundamentalist slot. I have, at times, put my faith in the historical reliability of the texts, while working hard to smooth over their internal contradictions; at other times I have tried to demythologise them or, to be more accurate, remythologise them, by separating the essence of the message from its cultural context and trying to universalise it. Today I believe that the significance of the texts cannot lie in historical claims about their extrinsic or revealed authority, but can only lie in their intrinsic ability to challenge and exalt us. This way of using them sees them as powerful archetypes that connect us with our own nature, its needs and confusions, offering us the wisdom and the discomfort of constant challenge. This way of using the texts, though it tries to understand as much as it can of their original context, effectively separates them from it and lets them speak to our condition in ways *we* can use. What the texts say to us will vary enormously in its usefulness, but it is the testimony of millions that the central core of the meaning and message of Jesus still offers a powerful instrument for guiding our lives today. In short, in the New Testament we can still find a usable past, but it has to be interpreted and adapted to our own needs.

An interesting paradox is that the aspect of Jesus that, on the face of it, is most likely to puzzle and alienate us may well be the one that challenges us most powerfully. The best way to enter the issue is to think about the word that many people regard as a kind of surname of the man of Nazareth, *Christ*. Christ is a Greek translation of the Hebrew word *messiah* meaning 'anointed', which denoted a person invested by God with specific powers and functions. In the Hebrew Scriptures it could refer to anyone set apart for a special task, such as a priest; but it was used particularly of the king, who was thought of as having been anointed by divine command. When the prophet Samuel was looking for a successor to the disgraced King Saul he discovered David and anointed him. David became the once and future king of Israel, the figure the people of Israel looked back on and longed for as they endured their own tragic history. Once or twice in this book I have looked briefly at this apocalyptic theme in scripture. I pointed out that apocalyptic is a widespread phenomenon among broken people, who project their anger and longing for deliverance onto a future hope of supernatural intervention. In ancient Israel part of that longing was for the coming of a righteous ruler, a son of David the ideal king, who would establish justice on earth. This messianic longing was an element in the brew of politics and religion in the time of Jesus, and caused nervousness among the political and priestly rulers of the people. It is not absolutely clear whether Jesus claimed to be the messiah, but his followers certainly gave him the title and the word Christ occurs 500 times in the New Testament. He was certainly executed as a messianic pretender, as the ironic inscription above his cross signified: *'The King of the Jews'*.[4] The messianic consciousness of Jesus is one of the most contentious issues of New Testament study. The most powerful fact in the debate has to be that Jesus was clearly thought of by his followers as the messiah, albeit a suffering rather than a triumphant one. The earliest gospel, Mark, clearly makes this identification, though he insists that Jesus wanted his identity to remain a secret:

[8.27] Jesus went on with his disciples to the villages of Caesarea Philippi; and on the way he asked his disciples, 'Who do people say that I am?' [28] And they answered him, 'John the Baptist; and others, Elijah; and still others, one of the prophets.' [29] He asked them, 'But who do you say that I am?' Peter answered him, 'You are the Messiah.' [30] And he sternly ordered them not to tell anyone about him.

[31] Then he began to teach them that the Son of Man must undergo great suffering, and be rejected by the elders, the chief priests, and the scribes, and be killed, and after three days rise again. [32] He said all this quite openly. And Peter took him aside and began to rebuke him. [33] But turning and looking at his disciples, he rebuked Peter and said, 'Get behind me, Satan! For you are setting your mind not on divine things but on human things.'

[34] He called the crowd with his disciples, and said to them, 'If any want to become my followers, let them deny themselves and take up their cross and follow me. [35] For those who want to save their life will lose it, and those who lose their life for my sake, and for the sake of the gospel, will save it. [36] For what will it profit them to gain the whole world and forfeit their life? [37] Indeed, what can they give in return for their life? [38] Those who are ashamed of me and of my words in this adulterous and sinful generation, of them the Son of Man will also be ashamed when he comes in the glory of his Father with the holy angels.'

Whatever the consciousness of Jesus on the matter, he was clearly understood by his immediate followers in messianic terms, and the fact that the early Church was in daily expectation of his return at the Second Coming lends weight to the apocalyptic interpretation of Jesus. One of the most famous theological texts of the twentieth century defined him as an ultimately tragic figure whose apocalyptic consciousness impelled him to his death. Albert Schweitzer believed that there was little apocalyptic excitement in the time of Jesus, apart from the movement that surrounded himself and John the Baptist.

It cannot be said that we know anything about the Messianic expectations of the Jewish people at that time.

On the contrary, the indifference shown by the Roman administration towards the movement proves that the Romans knew nothing of a condition of great and general Messianic excitement among the Jewish people. What is really remarkable about this wave of apocalyptic enthusiasm (which grew from the work of the Baptist and Jesus) is the fact that it was called forth not by external events, but solely by the appearance of two great personalities, and subsides with their disappearance, without leaving among the people generally any trace, except a feeling of hatred towards the new sect.

The Baptist and Jesus . . . set the times in motion by acting, by creating eschatological facts.

There is silence all around. The Baptist appears, and cries: 'Repent, for the Kingdom of Heaven is at hand.' Soon after that comes Jesus, and in the knowledge that He is the coming Son of Man lays hold of the wheel of the world to set it moving on that last revolution which is to bring all ordinary history to a close. It refuses to turn, and He throws Himself upon it. Then it does turn; and crushes him. Instead of bringing in the eschatological conditions, He has destroyed them. The wheel rolls onward, and the mangled body of the one immeasurably great Man, who was strong enough to think of Himself as the spiritual ruler of mankind and to bend history to his purpose, is hanging upon it still.[5]

More recent scholars have taken some of the intensity out of Schweitzer's claim, and added a more political dimension to the eschatology of Jesus. Since our search is for usable wisdom, not scholarly solutions, we can leave that debate aside and concentrate on its significance for our own time. The enduring value of apocalyptic is that it expresses radical discontent with the world as it is, so it can be used in the creatively subversive way that is essential if societies are not to be dominated and exploited by those who control the system and make sure they benefit from it. Jesus himself did not exclusively rely on the expectation of an eruption of the future into the present; he offered an eschatological manifesto for a new society now.

[5:1] When Jesus saw the crowds, he went up the mountain; and after he sat down, his disciples came to him. [2] Then he began to speak, and taught them, saying:

[3] 'Blessed are the poor in spirit, for theirs is the kingdom of heaven.

[4] 'Blessed are those who mourn, for they will be comforted.

[5] 'Blessed are the meek, for they will inherit the earth.

[6] 'Blessed are those who hunger and thirst for righteousness, for they will be filled.

[7] 'Blessed are the merciful, for they will receive mercy.

[8] 'Blessed are the pure in heart, for they will see God.

[9] 'Blessed are the peacemakers, for they will be called children of God.

[10] 'Blessed are those who are persecuted for righteousness' sake, for theirs is the kingdom of heaven.

[11] 'Blessed are you when people revile you and persecute you and utter all kinds of evil against you falsely on my account. [12] Rejoice and be glad, for your reward is great in heaven, for in the same way they persecuted the prophets who were before you.

[38] 'You have heard that it was said, "An eye for an eye and a tooth for a tooth." [39] But I say to you, Do not resist an evildoer. But if anyone strikes you on the right cheek, turn the other also; [40] and if anyone wants to sue you and take your coat, give your cloak as well; [41] and if anyone forces you to go one mile, go also the second mile. [42] Give to everyone who begs from you, and do not refuse anyone who wants to borrow from you.

[43] 'You have heard that it was said, "You shall love your neighbor and hate your enemy." [44] But I say to you, Love your enemies and pray for those who persecute you, [45] so that you may be children of your Father in heaven; for he makes his sun rise on the evil and on the good, and sends rain on the righteous and on the unrighteous. [46] For if you love those who love you, what reward do you have? Do not even the tax collectors do the same? [47] And if you greet only your brothers and sisters, what more are you doing than others? Do not even the Gentiles do the same? [48] Be perfect, therefore, as your heavenly Father is perfect.'

These verses are from the Sermon on the Mount in Matthew's gospel, one of the most subversely difficult passages in spiritual literature. We know from other places in the New Testament that Jesus subverted the law by exaggerating its claims to the point of absurdity. Custom and law are the basis of civilisation. Though they vary enormously from culture to culture, the role of custom is itself constant, acting as a container for the anarchic impulses of humanity. As we have already noticed, these customary systems can harden into a form that destroys their original usefulness. The best approach to religious codes that have become rigid and absolute is to acknowledge their arbitrariness and use them, if we use them at all, as a private discipline for ordering our own chaos. When they are proclaimed as the bearer of absolute and unchanging truth, defended in the traditional way, they enslave the human spirit rather than protect it from its own excesses. Jesus' vision burned through the external systems to the anxious human heart that lay beneath them and called for its transformation into a perfection of love. It is the impossibility of the vision, its eschatological hopelessness, that is the most compelling thing about it. Law has always been a problem for humanity. We need it to limit and discipline our tendency to excess and chaos, but it is in constant danger of becoming tyrannous and inflexible. When its detailed observance becomes the very purpose of our humanity, its dangerous stupidity needs to be subverted. The subversive intention of Jesus was probably expressed most succinctly when he warned his followers that they could not become his disciples unless they were prepared to hate their fathers and mothers. This profoundly counter-cultural challenge undermined the importance of tradition in creating human stability because it recognised its ultimately stifling effect on the creativity of the individual. Jesus is not offering us an election manifesto in the Sermon on the Mount; his purpose may not be programmatic so much as subversively ironic. He understands the necessity of law and its origin in our fear of the chaos of our own undisciplined passions; but he also recognises that the law itself can only shackle, never transform the passions; and it is the transformed heart that is his ambition because it alone can change the world. That is probably why he was loved by those whose sins were those of passion rather than of cruel control; he recognised in them a generosity and excess that was closer to his understanding of the nature of God than were the gaolers of the human spirit. This is probably the meaning of the parable of the talents, where the man buried his master's money rather than risk its loss by venturing it. This tension re-appears in the parable of the prodigal son, where the passionate nature that led to the excesses of the profligate brother does not finally prevent him from recognising the unconditional love of the welcoming father; whereas the disciplined control of

the older brother may possibly have stood in the way
of his understanding of the father's love, a point that is
never resolved because the parable is unfinished, probably
because it is presented as a permanent challenge to us all.
Something of the spirituality of human excess is captured
in the Borges poem about the penitent thief:

> O friends, the innocence of this friend
> Of Jesus! That simplicity which made him,
> From the disgrace of punishment, ask for
> And be granted Paradise
>
> Was what drove him time
> And again to sin and bloody crime.[6]

The human dilemma is that we stumble between excess
and deprivation in our self-management. We are animals,
and our tendency is to the undiscriminating satisfaction of
our natural impulses, as the life-force in all its cruel indifference pours through us. The mystery of consciousness
has brought awareness of our condition to us, and we
have learned to build hedges against our own appetites
and limits to our own cruelties. But we pay a price
in self-consciousness and the stifling of spontaneity; we
shuttle between sins of indulgence and sins of the spirit.
Controlled societies may preserve order, but the price
they pay is often the crucifixion of the human passions
out of fear. We crucify what we fear, we condemn in
others what we most mistrust in our own hearts. This
dance between fascination and fear is an ancient theme
in religious systems. It accounts for the periodic frenzies
of internal persecution, as for instance in the innumerable
witchcraft purges that disfigure Christian history. What the

genius of Jesus penetrated to was the ambiguity of the law itself and the way it could operate as a cloak for spiritual cruelties that were austere and unattractive substitutes for the real passions. He called for a radical re-appraisal of the nature of law; he did not argue for its abolition, but for an honest recognition that it was contingent and relative, meant to protect not stifle human flourishing. Implicit in his denunciation of the cruelties of legalism was the ·recognition that passionate sinners were usually more in touch with their real nature than those who had buried it beneath the law. The motive for this kind of repression is understandable, however, because lawless humanity is capable of terrible excesses. The point to remember is that the systems that are created to contain the excesses can themselves become excessive, so they require the constant criticism of the prophetic imagination. The eschatological vision of Jesus for a transformed humanity that is based on a perfected heart is not something that lends itself to programmes that translate exactly into reality. The ideal human life would recognise the goodness of both passion and order and would follow a pattern of controlled passion. We would not kill off our nature and its force, but nor would we allow it to dominate and drive us to excess. One way of achieving this is through self-knowledge, the kind of knowledge that knows the truth of its own desires and speaks them honestly in its heart. The persecuting heart is the one that lies about its own longings and then crucifies them in others.

But the vision of Jesus is about more than personal integration; it is about social honesty and justice. His apocalyptic longing for a mended creation may not be something that lends itself to a precise programme; but it can bring passion to the task of finding policies that

will better the world. Throughout history there have been
many of these eschatologies of human equality; the fact
that they never entirely succeed nor entirely fail is the
main point. They act as a stimulus to the work that is
always to be done of bringing out of the chaos of desire
and greed some order of mercy and justice. The Sermon
on the Mount is not exactly translatable into complete
political practice, but it can act as a stimulus to aspiration;
it can create the sort of discontent that leads to action.
A transformed version of the Jesus tradition, adapted for
our day, would lay less emphasis on believing things about
Jesus and more emphasis on imitating Jesus. It would be a
practice system rather than a belief system. Of course, there
is a basic core of belief at the basis of any praxis, but it can
be kept simple and can be largely self-evidencing; we will
attempt to follow the practice because we believe it to be
good for us and for the world. The test of this faith will
not be the dogmatic purity of the metaphysical convictions
we hold in our minds concerning Jesus, but the evidence
our lives will offer of our commitment to his practice of
subversive love.

What is left of Christianity should be the practice of
the kind of love that subverts the selfishness of power,
whether it is the subtle power of spiritual or the brutal
power of political institutions. All concentrations of power
justify their ascendancy with theory, as well as with more
blatant methods. For instance, many spiritual institutions in
the world today, including most of the Christian churches,
still practise profound discrimination against women. Of
course, they do not understand their discriminatory practice in that way; they justify it as obedience to a higher
law. They have hardened a transitory social arrangement
that probably made sense in its day into something that

is now absolute law and makes no sense in ours. The most profound paradox of Christian institutions is that, in the name of the great subverter, they have hardened the residue of ancient social norms into absolute prohibitions. A similar dynamic is at work among the churches in other aspects of human sexuality, such as the treatment of homosexual people. Here, the cruelty of Christianity is astonishing, especially when we remember that Jesus was the great prophet of pity.

CHAPTER THIRTEEN

Unconquered Hope

Christianity has been described as a religion for slaves, and this was the main reason that Nietzsche despised it. He claimed that what he called 'slave morality' emerged from the resentful revolt of the weak against the strength of the noble and their ethic of ruthlessness. It is an insightful criticism, and I'd like to explore it briefly. Nietzsche was an etymologist, a student of language and its origins, and he was certain that many terms in common speech derived their original meaning from the ancient social order of the warrior aristocrat. The word 'noble', for instance, with its dual use, suggesting both an adjective meaning fine, admirable, and a noun conveying the idea of an elevated person, he compared with the word 'base', which suggests the opposite, both adjectivally and nominally. Nietzsche developed an interesting idea from this difference. He said that in early societies the warrior class created standards of value, of good and bad, by their own will: what they willed, how they acted, was good, hence the tag 'noble'; what was furthest from their way was bad, hence the tag 'base'. Here are his own words:

> The essential characteristic of a good and healthy aris-
> tocracy is that it experiences itself not as a function
> (whether of the monarchy or of the commonwealth)
> but as their meaning and highest justification – that it
> therefore accepts with a good conscience the sacrifice of
> untold human beings who, for its sake, must be reduced

and lowered to incomplete human beings, to slaves, to instruments. Their fundamental faith simply has to be that society must not exist for society's sake but only as the foundation and scaffolding on which a choice type of being is able to raise itself to its higher task and to a higher state of being (cf. the outlook of the heroes of the Iliad)[1] – comparable to those sun-seeking vines of Java – they are called Sipo Matador – that so long and so often enclasp an oak tree with their tendrils until eventually, high above it but supported by it, they can unfold their crowns in the open light and display their happiness.[2]

For Nietzsche, the Roman ideal was the greatest exemplification of this warrior morality of power. He had an enormous admiration for these exemplars of the will to live, with their capacity for ruthlessness and their ability to be cruel, not necessarily for its own sake, but in order to keep their place at the top of the tree. This drive to lord it over others clearly has its origins in the sheer will to live and rule that marks the dominant male in the animal species. There is an obvious line between the warlike behaviour of the alpha male among primates, who have to battle to achieve and maintain supremacy, and the warrior leaders in early societies who lived by conquest and assertion. There is a passage in George Steiner's *Errata* which perfectly captures this warrior ethic and its sublime cruelty. He describes how his father read to him a translation of Homer's *Iliad* from Book XXI, and he continues:

Crazed by the death of his beloved Patroclus, Achilles is butchering the fleeing Trojans. Nothing can impede his homicidal fury. One of Priam's sons crosses his path. The wretched Lycaon has just returned from Lemnos to help defend his father's imperilled city. Earlier, Achilles had captured him and sold him into slavery at Lemnos, thus ironically consigning him to safety. But Lycaon is back. Now the appalled youth recognises the blind horror storming at him.[3]

Steiner reads what happens next from Robert Fagle's version of the Iliad:

> . . . He ducked, ran under the hurl
> And seized Achilles' knees as the spear shot past his back
> and stuck in the earth, still starved for human flesh.
> And begging now, one hand clutching Achilles' knees,
> the other gripping the spear, holding for dear life,
> Lycaon burst out with a winging prayer: 'Achilles!
> I grasp your knees – respect me, show me mercy!
> I am your suppliant, Prince, you must respect me!
> And it's just twelve days that I've been home in Troy –
> all I've suffered!
> But now again some murderous fate has placed me in
> your hands, your prisoner twice over – Father Zeus must
> hate me, giving me back to you! Ah, to a short life you
> bore me, mother, mother . . .
> Listen, this too, take it to heart, I beg you –
> don't kill me! I'm not from the same womb as Hector,
> Hector who killed your friend, your strong, *gentle* friend!'

Steiner goes on: 'At which line, my father stopped with an air of considered helplessness . . . . What, in God's name, happens next?' His father took up the original Greek text and, placing his son's finger at the place, translated what came next from the mouth of Achilles:

> . . . 'Fool,
> don't talk to me of ransom. No more speeches.
> Before Patroclus met his day of destiny, true,
> it warmed my heart a bit to spare some Trojans:

[201]

droves I took alive and auctioned off as slaves.
But now not a single Trojan flees his death,
not one the gods hand over to me before your gates,
none of all the Trojans, sons of Priam least of all!
Come, friend, you too must die. Why moan about it so?
Even Patroclus died, a far, far better man than you.
And look, you see how handsome and powerful I am?
The son of a great man, the mother who gave me life
a deathless goddess. But even for me, I tell you,
death and the strong force of fate are waiting.
There will come a dawn or sunset or high noon
when a man will take my life in battle too –
flinging a spear perhaps
or whipping a deadly arrow of his bow.'
Whereupon, Achilles slaughters the kneeling Lycaon.

Steiner continues, 'I recall graphically the rush of wonder, of a child's consciousness troubled and uncertainly
ripened, by that single word "friend" in the midst of the
death-sentence: "Come, friend, you too must die." And by
the enormity, so far as I could gauge it, of the question:
"Why moan about it so?"'[4]

In that passage we hear, in Achilles, the authentic voice
of heroic morality, the ethic of the strong men who create
good and bad by their own choices, and are not weakened
by self-doubt and the bite of conscience. There is another
passage in Nietzsche that talks about the strong man's
ability to forget and just get on with confronting the
challenges of life:

To be incapable of taking one's enemies, one's accidents,
even one's misdeeds seriously for very long – that is the
sign of strong, full natures in whom there is an excess of
power to form, to mould, to recuperate and to forget (a
good example of this is Mirabeau, who had no memory for

insults and vile actions done him and was unable to forgive simply because he – forgot.)[5]. Such a man shakes off with a single shrug many vermin that eat deep into others; here alone genuine 'love of one's enemies' is possible – supposing it to be possible at all on earth. How much reverence has a noble man for his enemies! – and such reverence is a bridge to love.[6]

For Nietzsche, the origin, what he called the genealogy, of morals and the guilty conscience comes in the transition to more organised social systems from this state of instinctive ascendance by the strong over all that opposed them in the struggle of life. The most fundamental change in human history occurred when the ascendant warrior, who defined reality and value by his own will, found himself enclosed within the walls of society and of peace. The cruel energies of the strong were then turned in upon themselves. Instincts that do not discharge themselves outwardly turn inward. Society created instruments of control, mainly the exercise of punishment, to protect itself against the old instincts, and thereby turned these instincts back against their possessors. 'Hostility, cruelty, joy in persecuting, in attacking, in change, in destruction – all this turned against the possessors of such instincts: that is the origin of the "bad conscience".'[7] Of course, the lordly and warlike instincts of original man were not entirely expunged by the emergence of political society; they evolved into the right of the aristocracy or nobility to rule, seen at its most complete in the Roman ideal, with its strong sense of its own right to dominate and order the world. There was a glorious cruelty about such absolute self-confidence. At its best it brought order to chaotic societies, but at a great cost to those at the bottom of the system. This is where the slave morality, which Nietzsche despised, emerged from, abetted by the spirit of Christianity, which substituted *pity* for the cruelty that characterised the ethos of the warrior system. Once this new ethos became dominant it added a further twist to the bite of conscience because it imposed a sense of divine disapproval upon the instinctive life itself. This is the origin of the ancient accusation against Christianity that it is against life and in love with death, the death of the passions, the death of ambition, the death of the drive of nature in all its exultant intensity. The further accusation is made that, since these drives never can be killed, they are merely covered in the gorgeous robes of priestly Christianity. The priest replaces the warrior, or becomes the warrior's adversary, and replaces the culture of ascendant cruelty with a culture of guilt and consolation.

If we accept Nietzsche's analysis, however critically, is it fair to associate Jesus with slave morality, with this depressive and resentful reaction of the weak against the strong? It is easy to romanticise the morality of the strong, the morality of the lion. Towards the end of his life Karl Marx was asked by an American journalist to answer the question: '"What is?" . . . to which . . . he replied: "Struggle!" At first it seemed as though I had heard the echo of despair but peradventure it was the law of life.'8 It is true that in this universe of struggle it is the strong who overcome, the swift who win the race. There is even a glory about watching the lion bring down its prey in one of those nature films that so enthral and appal us. The difference between us and the magnificent instinctiveness of the lion is that we have become conscious of ourselves and the consequences of our actions, so our conscience begins to make cowards of us. When we contemplate the misery of the mass of humanity down the ages, we can be overwhelmed by pity, the emotion Nietzsche despised; but it can be an angry pity, a pity that girds us for a different kind of struggle, the struggle to transform the human community so that the triumph of the strong is no longer based upon the immisiration of the weak. This is also a kind of war that calls for warriors with fortitude, and Jesus was undoubtedly a man of courage and resistance.

The question is, how was that resistance expressed? Dominic Crossan points out that in oppressive systems there is *always* resistance, overt and covert. He places Jesus on the borderline between the covert and overt arts of resistance to the system that oppressed the peasant class from which he came. He writes:

> What Jesus was doing is located exactly on the borderline between the covert and the overt arts of resistance. It was not, of course, as open as the acts of protesters, prophets, bandits, or messiahs. But it was more open than playing dumb, imagining revenge, or simply recalling Mosaic or Davidic ideals. His eating and healing were, in theory and practice, the precise borderline between private and public, covert and overt, secret and open resistance. But it was not less resistance for all of that.[9]

He did not preach armed rebellion; he did not call the people into the wilderness to wait for the supernatural intervention of the messiah who would cast down the mighty from their seats; what he set out to do was to build up the fragmented morale of a broken people, and to persuade them to live a life of resistance to the system that oppressed them, *by acting as if it had no real authority over them*. He followed the path of *organic* resistance, the building of a community that would strengthen the weak in their struggle against their dominators. This was the principle that, nineteen hundred years later, Marx would acknowledge, when he wrote: 'Social reforms are never carried out by the weakness of the strong; but always by the strength of the weak.'[10] Jesus was a strengthener of the weak. I shall come back to Marx, the last of the prophets; meanwhile, let me offer a summary at this point.

If we accept the main elements of the Darwinian understanding of nature, we can see how inevitable and important the emergence of the warrior class was in the evolution of our own species. As human structures became more complex and settled, the instinctive cruelty of the warrior was internalised, and there emerged the reflective adult who is caught in the struggle between instinct and responsibility, between the will to power of the individual and the needs of the community. Here we begin to see the emergence of the challenge to naked power, and it is always made by those at the bottom of the social pyramid. One of the interesting contrasts with the Darwinian ethic of power is the ethic of the Sermon on the Mount, which we looked at in the last chapter, and which turns the values of the warrior class on their head. I did not say that the ethic of Jesus destroyed the ethic of the warrior class; rather, it applied its courage and strength in the cause of the weak. From its beginnings Christianity has been profoundly counter-cultural, if by culture we mean the unchallenged ascendance of the instinctual life, leading to the domination of the weak by the strong. The thing to note about this revolt of the slaves is that it calls for immense courage, so Nietzsche was being perverse when he dismissed it. However, we probably ought to concede that the Church, as it became a power among other powers, replaced the honest domination by the strong with the covert domination by priestly Christendom. The work of Jesus, as a figure of contradiction and resistance to oppressive power, has been crucial in human development; and I want to end this chapter with an analysis of where we are in that process of evolution. It gives me an opportunity to bring the third of Steiner's great disturbers of human complacency, Karl Marx, into the discussion.

Marx was one of the most searching diagnosticians of the human condition. He may have been a lousy therapist, and no society today really tries to follow his prescriptions, but his diagnosis of human social pathology is still powerful and searching. His main insights, like most brilliant perceptions, are startlingly simple. One of his central claims is that power always justifies itself, not necessarily by brute force, though it is rarely reluctant to do that, but by theories or ideas. That is why the ruling ideas in any era always justify the position of the ruling class; these ideas are always used to make legitimate the way things are done by the people in charge. And what they are in charge of does not, for the moment, matter: it can be anything, from a whole nation down to a university or a hospital or a school or a family. It is important to understand that this is not necessarily an accusatory insight. A moment's thought will show how obvious and necessary it is for any institution to be able to justify itself to itself, if it is to continue to operate effectively and not paralyse itself into critical gridlock. The importance of the Marxist insight is that, by helping us to understand how institutions work, it puts us in a better position to strive for their improvement, or, where necessary, their complete subversion. Marx saw that human groups develop ideologies, views of the world and of their place in it, which serve their own interests and express their partial and incomplete point of view. He saw this as a process of false-consciousness:

Hitherto men have constantly made up for themselves false conceptions about themselves, about what they are and what they ought to be. They have arranged their relationships according to their ideas of God, of normal man, etc. The phantoms of their brains have gained the mastery over them. They, the creators, have bowed down before their creatures. Let us liberate them from the chimeras, the ideas, dogmas, imaginary beings under the yoke of which they are pining away.[11]

Jesus also warned us against false-consciousness when he told us that we are all more likely to see the speck in our brother's eye rather than the beam that is in our own. Since we rarely do catch on to our own false-consciousness, it is worth reminding ourselves of blatant examples from history that might at least induce some caution in us. Those of us who admire the sanity and moderation of the philosopher Aristotle also have to acknowledge the fact that he developed a theoretical justification for slavery because it was in the economic self-interest of the ruling class in ancient Greece, the class to which he belonged. Those of us who admire the sanity and moderation of the theologian Thomas Aquinas, himself a great lover of Aristotle, have to acknowledge that he gave divine sanction to absolute monarchy and serfdom because it was in the economic self-interest of the leaders of thirteenth-century Europe to do so. This attitude hung around for a long time in Christian theology, and was popularly expressed in Mrs Alexander's well-known hymn,

> The rich man in his castle,
> The poor man at his gate,
> God made them high or lowly,
> And ordered their estate.[12]

[208]

The tell-tale phrase is 'God made them high or lowly', and it is important to note that there is no relativising comma after, 'God made them'. We are told that 'God made them high or lowly', established them in an order that was fixed and unalterable. In other words, the division of society into classes, into the rich and into the poor, is not an accident of history or the result of straightforward exploitation of the weak by the strong: it is the way *God* has designed things. Tough if you drew the short straw, but who are you to criticise your maker? This kind of philosophical justification of the right to dominate others is the homage that the guilty conscience pays to the protest of the weak against the oppressive privileges of the strong. The powerful no longer have the honest courage to assert themselves by virtue of their own strength; instead, they now have to justify themselves by theory. This is the real hypocrisy of powerful elites, and the thing that makes them morally inferior to the old warriors who ruled by power alone, and rejoiced in it.

If ruling elites always consolidate their position by creating doctrinal justifications for it, how does social evolution ever occur? Where does the impetus to move on and challenge accepted values come from? Hegel would have answered that the spirit of history itself, the mystical reality that animates the whole of time, evolves gradually towards human liberty, away from the rule of naked force. Marx borrowed the evolutionary idea, but said that it worked itself out through changes in the means of production, creating greater social complexity and an accompanying misery and despair that provoked challenge and change. We don't have to buy the mysticism to recognise that history has, in fact, worked out like that. The point I want to derive from this is that, at some moment during the evolution of any human institution, a challenge is made against its ruling ideas by those who are its victims. I was shown a poignant reminder of this struggle for reform some time ago in a house in Edinburgh. When the owner was installing a new kitchen, he found a child's boot stuck up inside the chimney, a reminder that in Victorian Edinburgh children were sent up chimneys to clean them. It was the legislation against child labour and the factory acts that put paid to that kind of exploitation, but the reforms were opposed every step of the way by those who profited from a system that virtually enslaved children. It is also worth remembering how opposed the Royal Colleges and the British Medical Association were to the emergence of the National Health Service in Britain, so that, to quote his own words, Aneuran Bevan had to stuff the mouths of the doctors with gold in order to get the main elements of his reforms through. In the United States today one of the strongest obstacles to the emergence of universal health provision is the American Medical Association, the group that protects the wealth of one of America's most selfish elites.

When they no longer have to maintain themselves simply by the application of the cruel will to power, ruling groups always disguise their own self-interest in the language of theory and necessity. An interesting example is provided by Kenneth Galbraith in his book, *The Good Society*.

> The rich have a certain reluctance in defending their wealth and income as a social, moral or divine right, so their only possible resort is the functional justification. From the undisturbed and admittedly unequal distribution of income comes the incentive to effort and innovation that is in the service of all. And from the income so

distributed come the saving and investment that are for the advantage of all. The rich and the affluent do not speak in defence of their own good fortune; they speak as the benign servitors of the common good. Some may even be embarrassed as to their worldly reward, but they suffer it, nonetheless, as a service to the general well-being. Social and economic purpose is adjusted to personal comfort and convenience.[13]

Galbraith is well aware of the efficacy of the market economy at generating wealth, but he is concerned at the way those who benefit from the system refuse to address the damaging effects it has on the most vulnerable members of society. This was also one of Marx's insights. He wrote: 'Pauperism forms a condition of capitalist production, and of the capitalist development of wealth. It forms part of the incidental expenses of capitalist production: but capital usually knows how to transfer these from its own shoulders to those of the working class and the petty bourgeoisie.'[14] In his recent biography of Marx, Francis Wheen comments on this claim: 'In the context Marx is referring not to the pauperisation of the entire proletariat but to the "lowest sediment" of society – the unemployed, the ragged, the sick, the old, the widows and orphans. These are the incidental expenses which must be paid by the working population and the petty bourgeoisie. Can anyone deny that such an underclass still exists?'[15]

Most unprejudiced thinkers would acknowledge the failures as well as the successes of the global market economy. Few people today argue for its complete abolition. Increasingly, however, people are calling for a candid acknowledgement of its failures. 'We created the thing,' they say, 'so why can't we learn to modify or correct it?' And we have started doing this in certain areas. We have learnt comparatively recently about the cost to the planet of unregulated industrial activity, so we try to control businesses that pollute our rivers and destroy the quality of the air we breathe. So far, however, we are uncertain about how to respond to the adverse effects of the global market economy on the human environment. Since self-interest always justifies itself to itself, we should work hard at trying to understand how the system that benefits us consequentially damages or destroys many other lives in the process. The word that Jesus used to describe this process is, in Greek, *metanoia*. It is usually, and misleadingly, translated as *repentance;* it actually means a deep switch in thinking of the sort that racists have to go through, if they are to change their attitude towards people of other races; or misogynists, if they are to change their attitude towards women; or homophobes, if they are to shift their attitudes towards gay and lesbian people. All transformation starts in this painful process of radical re-appraisal. And the main fact we have to acknowledge is that the system that has made most of us more prosperous has plunged a significant proportion of our fellow citizens into poverty and despair.

One of the most tragically enduring facts of the history of human industry is that change in the methods of production always has a disproportionate impact upon the most vulnerable in society. History, like nature, seems to be indifferent to the pain it causes the weak. We can see this in the way the Industrial Revolution chewed up and spat out generations of the poor, before we learned how to protect them from its worst depredations. The paradox of our time is that it is the death of heavy industry that is now devastating the poor. Much of this is the consequence of global economic changes, coupled with the closure of pits and heavy industries. Heavy industry has been replaced by the knowledge economy, and we are only now trying to catch up with its consequential impact upon the poor and ill-educated. And, as if that were not enough, social change has combined with the economic revolution to destroy the cultural cohesion of the most vulnerable sections of our society. When the culture revolutions of the 1960s met and married the economic revolution of the 1980s, there was created a potent instrument of social change that has transformed the social landscape of the West, and its most devastating impact has been upon young, ill-educated workless males. The institutions that once gave them a motive for responsible living, such as holding down a tough, demanding job with its own culture and honour, and presiding, however clumsily, within a marriage and family that was the primary context for the nurture and socialising of children, have largely disappeared, and with them the main ways the human community traditionally disciplined and integrated what the Prayer Book calls 'the unruly wills and affections of sinful men'. This shattering of the structures that once gave the poor significance and purpose has created a breeding ground for despair that prompts the kind of destructive behaviour that continually reinforces their alienation. Whenever I refer to these facts in certain circles someone inevitably points out that no one in Britain is starving today because absolute poverty has been eradicated. That may be technically true, but minority poverty has an exclusionary cruelty that is all its own. When most people were poor there was a camaraderie and cultural cohesion in belonging to the working class that gave them a strength and pride that transcended the structures that excluded them. In a society where most people are prosperous, and the poor are a minority whose culture has disintegrated, the pain and anger they feel is heightened. To use the Nietzschean vocabulary, these are the slaves of today's system, but they are so demoralised that their anger is turned mainly upon themselves. They represent the greatest moral challenge of our time.

We have come a long way from the heroic cruelty of Achilles, but the same dynamic of power is still at work in the human community. It presents to Christians the same challenge as of old, though in subtler forms. Those who follow the way of Jesus are still called to the same task of resistance and transformation. The instruments they use may be different, their weapons may be intellectual challenge and protest rather than the direct action that characterised revolutionary change in the past, but the end is the same – to uncover God's justice on earth. One of the traditional terms for this process is 'the principle of fraternity'. Richard Rorty says of it:

> Fraternity is an inclination of the heart, one that produces a sense of shame at having much when others have little. It is not the sort of thing that anybody can have a theory about or that people can be argued into having. Perhaps the most vivid description of the American concept of fraternity is found in a passage from John Steinbeck's 1939 novel *The Grapes of Wrath*. Steinbeck describes a desperately impoverished family, dispossessed tenant farmers from Oklahoma, camped out at the edge of Highway 66, sharing their food with an even more desperate migrant family. Steinbeck writes: '"I have a little food" plus "I have none." If from this problem the sum is "We have a little food," the movement has direction.' As long as people in trouble can sacrifice to help people who are in still worse trouble, Steinbeck insisted, there is fraternity, and therefore social hope.[16]

This is what is left of the apocalyptic hope and it calls us from self-obsession to work for the justice on earth that is never here but is always on its way, always coming. Marx was another prophet whose prediction failed but whose hope for a just order in the world is as potent now as it ever was. We should not be afraid to admit that Christianity is a religion of failed prophecies; the more important truth is that it is a religion of unconquerable hope. The only miracle that matters is the fact that a universe driven by a power that is indifferent to the creatures it produces so prodigally and discards so effortlessly should give birth to such an overwhelming pity for its own victims.

CHAPTER FOURTEEN

Rewinding the Past

In this book I am trying to reclaim three revolutionary elements from what is left of the spirit of Jesus. In chapter 12 I tried to uncover the challenge of Jesus to human systems that are allowed to harden into tyrannous absolutes. In the last chapter I pointed to the angry pity of Jesus and the endless challenge of social hope. I want now to look at what was perhaps the most distinctive of his teachings, forgiveness.

There is a fundamental distinction to be made in the meaning of the word *authority*. The more obvious or usual meaning suggests *extrinsic authority*. This refers to an individual, agency or institution that has power over us and can compel our obedience. Many of these extrinsic authorities operate in a relatively benign and helpful way. The traffic police officer has authority or power over us in the highly specific situation of traffic discipline. We may feel that he is performing the task in an incompetent way or that he is giving preference to the stream of traffic coming in the opposite direction to the one we are going in, but we are unlikely to challenge his authority by getting out of the car and taking over his role. Most of us are tolerant of minor versions of extrinsic authority, although, in our encounters with officialdom, we often experience examples of petty tyranny of the sort that makes us expostulate to our friends afterwards. It is altogether different if we live in a real tyranny, in one of those authoritarian societies where people are generally ordered around in ways that those of us who live in liberal democracies would find intolerable. Even worse are the totalitarian societies where there is no aspect of life that is beyond the prying interference of rulers and their brutal officials. In these cultures, outward conformity to the powers that be is often combined with an inward withdrawal of consent, so that the soul of the apparently compliant individual maintains a sort of spiritual purity. Sometimes women who have been raped offer a similar kind of testimony. They were subjected to extrinsic power, brute strength was imposed upon them, but they did not offer it the consent of their hearts and minds and tried to preserve a detachment from it that separated them from the horrifying thing that was happening to them.

Very different from extrinsic or imposed authority is *intrinsic authority*. Intrinsic authority wins our inner consent by a charismatic appeal that persuades and draws affirmation from us. We say Yes to it, acknowledge that it has a legitimate claim upon us, has caused a powerful act of recognition and mutuality to work within our hearts and minds. To use another sexual analogy, we fall in love and open ourselves to the entrance of the other, consent eagerly to the other's embrace, participate fully in the encounter. They said of Jesus that *he spoke with authority, and not as the scribes*. I am assuming that this means he had an intrinsic authority that called forth voluntary assent from people, while the scribes had an extrinsic authority that extracted official compliance, but never real inward assent to what was said or commanded by them. And we have all had experiences of this sort. There have been times, for instance, when we have had to listen to a speech delivered, say, by a minister in one of the departments of government. It is quite obvious to us that the speech has been written for him, that it is not his own in any way that compels our interest, and we listen politely, fulfilling one of the rituals of public life in that unengaged way that usually characterises such occasions. It is very different, however, if we go to hear a lecture by a brilliant and charismatic scholar whose command of her subject draws admiring approval from us. The speaker and the speech have an intrinsic authority that draws attention from us.

The distinction between extrinsic and intrinsic authority is very important in our encounter with religious meaning. We have all sat under clergy who had no intrinsic authority, no ability to compel our assent, no matter how loaded they were with the trappings of extrinsic authority. And we encounter the same distinction when we deal with religious language and the claims of religious authority. The mere assertion of authority does nothing for us. For instance, the claim that a particular statement must have authority in our lives because it happens to be in the Bible is likely to leave many of us cold. No form of words will impress us because of their claim to extrinsic authority; a platitude is still a platitude, even if it comes from a prime minister or an archbishop. But their words might impress, challenge or console us, if they had the charisma of intrinsic power and not because of who uttered them. They might draw recognition and assent from us because of their self-evidencing authority. 'They have something,' we say, 'they got to us, touched us, made us shiver.' This distinction in the way we understand the meaning of authority is very important when we are trying to find usable wisdom from religious narratives and traditions. The Christian tradition claims that Jesus was a manifestation of God, God made accessible in a human life. No matter what we make of the claim itself – and it is hardly one that can be vindicated by the standard tests of verifiability, so it must always remain a claim of faith – the very fact of the emergence of the claim is itself interesting and significant and suggests, at the very least, that the presence and teaching of Jesus had a considerable impact upon those who met him. It seems safe to claim that the route to the extrinsic authority that was claimed for Jesus – that he came from God – must have first gone through the demonstrable fact of his intrinsic authority. I would like to suggest that it is more important to open ourselves to the words that gave rise to the claim of divinity, rather than to profess allegiance to the claim itself, but show little or no personal response to the words that precipitated it. It is more important to be forgiving than to claim that Jesus' attitude to forgiveness demonstrates his essential divinity.

If we follow the criterion of usefulness that I have been developing in this book, what use can we make of his teaching on forgiveness, one of the central elements in his teaching? In the model prayer he taught his disciples, they were to say 'forgive us our sins as we forgive those who sin against us'. In his parables he repeatedly taught the particular importance of remembering our own need for and experience of forgiveness when we ourselves are called upon to forgive.

It was E.M. Forster who said it, but it could as easily have been Jesus: 'Only connect.' Connecting in this radically magnanimous way is difficult, but Jesus was right to make it the central element in his teaching. Without radical forgiveness of one another, we condemn ourselves not only to the pain of our offences against one another, but to years of misery that deepen the original wound by the corrosions of bitterness and hatred. And this is true not only of our individual trespasses against one another, but of the sins of whole tribes and nations. Forgiveness is an art that politicians are only just beginning to work at, but their struggle to apply it to the some of the most intractable conflicts that disfigure the human situation today gives us an opportunity to meditate on a crucial but complex aspect of human relationships.

In an unpublished novel, John Whale describes one of the most difficult of human predicaments. Philip, the main character in the story, has gone into the country near Oxford to prepare for the death that cancer will soon bring to him. His predicament is that he has a sin on his conscience for which he believes there is no obvious forgiveness. His mother had been a monster of tyranny and intolerance all his life, but towards her end he had taken her into his home to care for till her death. Confused, doubly incontinent and enduringly spiteful, she maintained an iron grip on him and would permit no one else to assist in her care. One day he stopped feeding her, giving her, instead, occasional cups of hot water. She hardly noticed, and in a few days she was dead. Now Philip, contemplating his own impending death, is unable to find forgiveness. Who can forgive him? He cannot forgive himself. Though he is a priest, he is not quite sure if there is a God to forgive; and, anyway, can God forgive on his mother's behalf? This is where the predicament really bites: she who was sinned against is no longer available to offer the forgiveness that might heal his tortured heart.

This is a dramatic example of a not uncommon experience. Many innocent people feel guilt at the death of a loved one: did they do enough or did their neglect somehow contribute to the tragedy? And the comfort of friends does not really help, because the one person who might make a difference is no longer there to make it. The pain is crueller if something wrong *was* done, if there *was* some kind of culpable neglect. That is when guilt burns and gnaws at the gut and changes the beauty of the day into bleakness and sorrow. Bad as all of that is, it is not the difficulty that particularly obsesses me. I've had more to be forgiven for than to forgive in my life; nothing very terrible has happened to me, so I sometimes wonder if I have any right to talk about forgiveness at all. Has my message been too easy? I have preached about forgiveness a lot over the years, but would I be able to practise it if one of my children had been abducted and murdered or if they had been gassed in Auschwitz? How can anyone forgive in those circumstances? This brings us right up against the central dilemma. The world is dying for lack of forgiveness, but we don't want a forgiveness that cheapens the evil we do to one another; we don't want a forgiveness that denies the claims of justice or ignores the pain of that endless procession of victims.

This is tough enough on the individual level, but it becomes a thousand times worse when we try to think about situations where whole communities stare in unforgiving hatred at one another, as they still do in Northern Ireland, the Middle East and other places too numerous to list. Who is to do the forgiving there? How can it even start? All the sides have inflicted terrible wounds on one another, so how can anyone even begin the process? Who is to bring back the dead to speak the words of release and reconciliation? Wouldn't forgiveness cheapen the lives that have been lost and diminish the responsibility of those who took them? That is certainly what we hear whenever the Secretary of State for Northern Ireland releases another group of what their own side call political prisoners and the other side call terrorists. *Cheap grace* it has been called, this forgiving of others, this letting them off, this turning the other cheek. 'They should be brought to account, should pay for it, should burn in hell, should stay in gaol till they rot,' the voices cry, 'because they have taken joy away for ever from our lives.'

The inability or refusal to forgive is understandable, but it also seems to be a terrible mirror image of the punishment we hand out to the offenders. It keeps us in prison, as well as those who have victimised us, locked up in our own hatred, endlessly working the treadmill of our own bitter memories. That is certainly the impression we get when we look in on those intractable disputes in Israel and Northern Ireland. We get a wearying sense of communities who are imprisoned in the pains of their own history; they are dying in their chains and unwilling to stand up and shake them off. The sight may frustrate us from the comparative calm of our own situation, but we can enter imaginatively in their minds if we try to feel the outrage caused by the death and maiming of loved ones during the long years of conflict. We would probably all agree that at some stage in the process the offence has to be admitted if the forgiving is to do its work on the one who needs it: surely we can't receive forgiveness till we acknowledge that we need it? Behind that claim lies the ancient human conviction that we are responsible for our own actions, have freedom, could have chosen otherwise. That's what gnaws at us in those times of guilt and remorse when we look back at our lives: a little more self-control here, a slight change of direction there, and things could have been different and we would not now be eaten up with regret.

All of that is true, and there could be no moral life if it were not true, but it is not the whole truth. The men who hammered the nails into the hands and feet of Jesus must have known what they were doing, must have had some responsibility, yet he prayed, 'Father forgive them, for they know not what they do.' Maybe he just meant the executioners, the ones who did the dirty work, not the real agents of the crime, Pilate and Caiaphas, but I doubt it. I think everyone was included in the forgiveness he prayed for, because he recognised that none of us is completely in charge of our lives. To a very great extent we were made what we are by factors that were not in our control. As we saw when we thought about the myth of original sin, much of what we are comes straight from our animal past. It is true that consciousness gives us some control over our instincts, but it is far from complete. We all know the experience of moral powerlessness: 'I couldn't help it,' we say, 'something got into me.' If this is true of many of our private choices, think how much truer it is when people get caught up in historical tragedies over which they have no control. If you had a bitter childhood in a Palestinian refugee camp it might make you what the world calls a terrorist. If you spent your boyhood in the divided streets of Belfast it might make you into the kind of man who could be persuaded to pick up the gun. Even Hannibal Lecter had a childhood that helped to form him into the monster he later became in the famous novels of Thomas Harris. We know how formative early childhood experience is in making us into what we later become, for better or for worse. When we think about it, therefore, the human situation is actually quite complicated. We know we are responsible for our own actions, have free will; but we also know that other people's choices have influenced and helped to form us, so our freedom is a qualified thing at best, and some people have been dealt a hand that hardly offers them any choices at all. I think that this is why Jesus was a strange combination of anger and compassion, as though he carried the pain of this tension in his own heart. He hated and challenged cruelty and its effects, but he had an enormous compassion for sinners and the helpless predicaments they found themselves in. He forgave the men who hammered in the nails, just as he had previously offered Pilate sympathy for having to condemn him to death. The paradox of the anger of Jesus was that it was poured out against those who refused to acknowledge any kind of fault, while to those who admitted the confusions of their lives he was filled with love and compassion. Perhaps forgiveness was so central to his message that he was made angry by those who denied themselves the opportunity to receive it by blindness to their own condition. Of course, we do not have a systematic treatment of the practice of forgiveness in Jesus, but all the elements we would require for such a treatment are present. What there can be no doubt about, however, is his conviction about the importance of forgiveness to everyone caught up in the old cycle of sorrow and pain.

We ought to leave the offender on one side for the moment and notice how important forgiveness is for the healing and growth of the forgiver. If there is no forgiving the wound of the original offence can keep growing till it takes over a whole life. This is what happened to a woman in the United States. Her daughter had been murdered, the killer had been caught and convicted and was awaiting execution on death row. The mother hated him with an all-consuming hatred and planned to be present at his execution. She also wanted to confront him before his death with the terrible thing he had done, so the prison authorities arranged for her to visit him. As she spoke to him on death row, on her first visit, she started crying. Then, unprompted and without intending to, she found herself forgiving him and a great weight fell from her. She no longer felt imprisoned in bitterness and hatred, no longer wanted her daughter's killer killed. She continued to visit him and one day, in tears, he confessed his guilt and asked for the forgiveness he had already been given. Since his execution she has been campaigning against capital punishment; and her life has been restored to her.

We should notice one or two things about this case. It was probably because he had already been forgiven that the killer was able to repent. The forgiveness melted his defences and helped him to see and own his crime for the first time. This is how the radical forgiveness that Jesus taught seems to work. In chapter 15 of Luke's gospel father of the prodigal son forgives his son before he can get a word of his prepared speech out, and it is that act of grace that melts his selfish heart into real repentance.

[11] Then Jesus said, 'There was a man who had two sons. [12] The younger of them said to his father, "Father, give me the share of the property that will belong to me." So he divided his property between them. [13] A few days later the younger son gathered all he had and traveled to a distant country, and there he squandered his property in dissolute living. [14] When he had spent everything, a severe famine took place throughout that country, and he began to be in need. [15] So he went and hired himself out to one of the citizens of that country, who sent him to his fields to feed the pigs. [16] He would gladly have filled himself with the pods that the pigs were eating; and no one gave him anything. [17] But when he came to himself

he said, "How many of my father's hired hands have bread enough and to spare, but here I am dying of hunger! [18] I will get up and go to my father, and I will say to him, 'Father, I have sinned against heaven and before you; [19] I am no longer worthy to be called your son; treat me like one of your hired hands.'" [20] So he set off and went to his father. But while he was still far off, his father saw him and was filled with compassion; he ran and put his arms around him and kissed him. [21] Then the son said to him, "Father, I have sinned against heaven and before you; I am no longer worthy to be called your son." [22] But the father said to his slaves, "Quickly, bring out a robe – the best one – and put it on him; put a ring on his finger and sandals on his feet. [23] And get the fatted calf and kill it, and let us eat and celebrate; [24] for this son of mine was dead and is alive again; he was lost and is found!" And they began to celebrate.

[25] 'Now his elder son was in the field; and when he came and approached the house, he heard music and dancing. [26] He called one of the slaves and asked what was going on. [27] He replied, "Your brother has come, and your father has killed the fatted calf, because he has got him back safe and sound." [28] Then he became angry and refused to go in. His father came out and began to plead with him. [29] But he answered his father, "Listen! For all these years I have been working like a slave for you, and I have never disobeyed your command; yet you have never given me even a young goat so that I might celebrate with my friends. [30] But when this son of yours came back, who has devoured your property with prostitutes, you killed the fatted calf for him!" [31] Then the father said to him, "Son, you are always with me, and all that is mine is yours. [32] But we had to celebrate and rejoice, because this brother of yours was dead and has come to life; he was lost and has been found."'[1]

I know this from my own experience. Judge and attack

me and I'll defend myself with anger and violence; offer me love and understanding and you'll break my heart into sorrow for the way I've hurt you. There is a beautiful example of this process at work in Helen Waddell's novel *Peter Abelard*. Abelard, a charismatic scholar in twelfth-century Paris, seduces Heloise, the niece of a colleague and friend. In a revenge attack, Abelard is castrated and goes into angry exile. Heloise goes into a convent, leaving their child with relatives, her love for Abelard undiminished. Brooding bitterly on his situation, Abelard is unable to give or receive forgiveness. Suddenly, out of nowhere, he hears in his head the words Jesus spoke to the woman taken in adultery:

> *'Neither do I condemn thee; go and sin no more.'* He stopped his trampling up and down the room. He did not know where the words had come from; he had been in no humour to call them to his mind, and suddenly they were in him, like a memory in his blood. His rage dropped from him, though a pulse was till beating in his cheek. He sat down, utterly exhausted, and dropped his head on his hands. 'And because He would not condemn me,' he thought, 'I could lay my head in the dust.'[2]

Forgiveness can release honesty in the offender; more importantly, it liberates the person who has been offended, so that she is no longer trapped, caught up in the continuing horror of the event, and can move away from it into a new future. It is easy to see *how* forgiveness works, but it is still hard to figure out how people find the generosity for great forgiving, for letting go of monstrous wrongs. This is why none of us has the right to call on other people to forgive, though we may be able to remind them that we are all, at times, in need of forgiveness and that those who refuse forgiveness may be destroying the bridge that one day they may themselves have to cross. Nevertheless, it is true that the most effective exponents of forgiveness are the ones who themselves have been wounded. Only the wronged can really preach forgiveness, only the crucified.

This is one reason why Christians say that the crucifixion of Jesus was a saving event, something that can bring healing to us in our broken humanity. At the centre of the maelstrom of violence and cursing we hear this voice offering forgiveness to us for all the things we have ignorantly or knowingly done. It is a voice that pleads with us to pause and reflect on the way our lives can be consumed by hatred and bitterness, so that the past, like an implacable tyrant, controls the present and destroys the future. 'Release yourselves from that bondage,' the voice on the cross says, 'lay down the burden of hatred, forgive; lay down the burden of guilt, accept forgiveness; and the future will be a new country.'

Though I am still a bit baffled about where people find the grace to forgive in the kind of horrifying circumstances we have been thinking about, it is increasingly clear to me how important forgiveness is to a healthy private life; even more importantly, it is essential in political life, especially in situations of chronic conflict. Who could ever pick their way through the ancient antagonisms of Northern Ireland or Israel/Palestine and produce an accurate check sheet of the rights and wrongs of those tragedies? It can never be done. The accounting mentality simply destines the tragedy to continue, unless there is forgiveness. Fortunately, there is one recent example of a concerted effort to make political forgiveness work. South Africa is a country whose history is drenched in blood and hatred, but a remarkable experiment called the

Truth Commission took place there, in which we saw the politics of forgiveness at work. It seemed to great souls like Mandela and Tutu that the only way to lay that terrible past to rest was not to forget it, but to guarantee forgiveness for those responsible for it. The Commission guaranteed amnesty for those who owned up to their offences, and created conditions in which the full horror of the past could be owned by both agents and victims, so that all could move on into the future. Great emphasis is still being placed upon the healing of memories, but that healing cannot happen if the truth of the past is not acknowledged and confronted. The report of the Truth Commission is full of examples of this process at work, as South Africa tries painfully to heal its past by the radical political application of the dynamic of forgiveness. The British politician Denis Healey wrote that you never reach conclusions in politics, but you do have to make decisions, you have to get on with things. The instinct for political forgiveness is close to that insight. It knows how complex our sins and mistakes are, and how impossible it is to draw up a true balance sheet. Forgiveness gives us the courage to deal with the business of the past, so that we can walk away from it at last, and move into the future. The philosopher who thought most deeply about the application of the idea of forgiveness to human communities was Hannah Arendt. She wrote:

And this is the simple fact that, though we don't know what we are doing when we are acting, we have no possibility ever to undo what we have done. Action processes are not only unpredictable, they are also irreversible; there is no author or maker who can undo, destroy, what he has done if he does not like it or when the consequences are disastrous. The possible redemption from the predicament of irreversibility is the faculty of forgiving, and the remedy

[229]

for unpredictability is contained in the faculty to make and keep promises. The two remedies belong together: forgiving relates to the past and serves to undo its deeds, while binding oneself through promises serves to set up in the ocean of future uncertainty islands of security without which not even continuity, let alone durability of any kind, would ever be possible in the relationships between men. Without being forgiven, released from the consequences of what we have done, our capacity to act would, as it were, be confined to one single deed from which we could never recover; we would remain the victim of its consequences for ever, not unlike the sorcerer's apprentice who lacked the magic formula to break the spell. Without being bound to the fulfilment of promises, we would never be able to achieve that amount of identity and continuity which together produce the 'person' about whom a story can be told; each of us would be condemned to wander helplessly and without direction in the darkness of his own lonely heart, caught in its ever changing moods, contradictions, and equivocalities. In this respect, forgiving and making promises are like control mechanisms built into the very faculty to start new and unending processes.[3]

The centrality of forgiveness, in the teaching of Jesus, and the new beginning it constantly affords us is his most liberating gift to humanity. It is why following Jesus is both joyful and serious. It is about the enjoyment of life and all its colour; it's a banquet, a wedding feast. But it's one to which everyone is invited and that takes work, and sometimes it's dangerous work, because there are many people at the party who don't want to let anyone else in and would, if they got their way, get rid of some who are already there. That is why those who try to use the example of Jesus have to learn to look at people differently,

to practise imaginative compassion, to see the world as it
might be and not simply accept it as it is. Seeing it that way
round is to see it the way he saw it; and if enough of us
start seeing it that way, why it might even come to pass.

CHAPTER FIFTEEN

For Love of the World

Whenever any new vision or idea is born, whether in religion, art or politics, it requires a process to carry it through history. The process is invented to mediate the vision, to make it present in time. Weber called this process, 'the routinisation of charisma'.[1] The great, gifted thing, the *charism*, has to be embodied in a routine, a mechanism, whether it is a political or religious movement. Two related and unavoidable things happen in this process of routinisation. By definition, visions or charisms cannot be perfectly routinised or institutionalised, so the very process that gives them continuing life also begins to kill them. That is bad enough; what amplifies this process of corruption is that the people who are brought in to direct the institution that carries the original vision are more interested in and are usually better at preserving the process than the purpose it is meant to serve. The process itself becomes fascinating and takes them over, so that its protection and maintenance becomes their primary purpose. Some echoes or remnants of the original vision still get through, of course, so the dangerous memory is preserved; but the main impulse becomes the survival of the institution itself. There is even a kind of tragic grandeur in the necessary corruption of institutions, if it is honestly admitted. Part of Abraham Lincoln's greatness as a human being was that he understood how necessary these tragic compromises were to the survival of societies. He wanted

[232]

to preserve the union of the states, without slavery if possible; but if the price of saving it was the retention of slavery, he was prepared to pay it. He was prepared to collude in the preservation of an obvious evil if it was the price of the survival of the nation: 'My paramount object in this struggle is to save the Union . . . If I could save the Union without freeing any slave, I would do it; and if I could save it by freeing some and leaving others alone, I would also do that . . . I have here stated my purpose according to my views of official duty and I intend no modification of my oft-expressed personal wish that all men everywhere could be free.'[2]

In Lincoln, as in some other leaders, there was a sense of the tragic grandeur of these necessary compromises with truth and justice, and one can salute those who have to make them. In the legend of the Grand Inquisitor in Dostoevsky's *Brothers Karamazov*[3] it is this very dilemma that the aged inquisitor describes to the imprisoned Jesus. During the Inquisition in Spain, when heretics are being burned at the stake, Jesus comes to Seville and walks through the city. People instinctively recognise him and seek his counsel, so the Grand Inquisitor has him arrested and comes to visit him in prison. He delivers a monologue to him in which he points out that people do not want the freedom Jesus brought them. They want the security of a power system, including all its necessary compromises. They will never be able to follow Christ's way of freedom and compassion. At the end of the old man's monologue Jesus says nothing, but he steps forward and kisses him 'gently on his bloodless, aged lips'.[4] He understands and forgives the tragic compromises leaders of nations and churches have to make.

I encountered something of the compromised heroism

of this approach during the Lambeth Conference of 1998. As I have already made clear, the most divisive subject on the agenda was homosexuality. The conference provided the world with an illuminated showcase for Christian homophobia and intolerance. The debate on the subject was an ugly affair; some of the bishops who voted against the condemnation of homosexuality that was passed by an enormous majority said they felt physically threatened by other bishops during the course of the virulent debate. A working compromise of some sort could have been achieved, but the Caiaphatic ethic prevailed, mainly because of the power of evangelical groups who constantly threaten to split the Church if any compromise on its traditional condemnation of homosexuality is suggested. After the debate, one English bishop, who had proved himself to be a man of courage in other areas, told me that he had decided to keep himself well below the parapet in this struggle because his imperative was to keep the Church of England together. This certainly seems to be the prevailing principle in the Church of England at the moment, where bishops are told to keep off the subject to avoid splitting the Church. The American Episcopal Church is the great hate object of evangelicals and much time is spent by the management of the Anglican Communion in appeasing their tantrums. The Church exists to preserve the dangerous memory of a man who warned us against the idolatrous power that places its own survival before pity and truth, but it long ago gave up the attempt to order itself by the sublime impossibility of his vision.

But the imposture goes deeper than the inevitable compromises of institutional survival. It goes down into the Church's theological system, which has created as profound a departure from Jesus as the Church's collusion

with power. I want to open up this subject by referring to
a book on feminist philosophical theology, Grace Jantzen's
Becoming Divine.[5] Basing herself on the thought of Hannah
Arendt, Jantzen suggests that we need to develop a new set
of theological symbols if Christianity is to be a movement
that affirms rather than denies life. She meditates on the
significant fact that, in the Western tradition, humans are
described as *mortals*, and the task of the Church is to
secure their immortality by programmes of 'redemption'
or 'salvation'. The basic premise is that this life is of little
significance in itself, but is only a prelude to a state beyond
life that is either one of weal or of woe. We are mortal,
born to die, and it is what awaits us beyond death that
should pre-occupy our every breath, since the way we
use this life will procure either an immortality of bliss
or an immortality of woe. Hannah Arendt scorned this
pre-occupation with death and proposed a new symbolism
that emphasised not the inevitability of our dying, but the
actuality of our living. She wanted us to think of ourselves,
not as *mortals*, as those who will die, but as *natals*, as those
who are alive; and she wanted us to act for love not hatred
of the world. Borrowing this distinction, Jantzen wants us
to emphasise our natality, rather than our mortality, and
to celebrate and use the life we have now rather than
waste it in morbid preparations for life after death. In her
exposition of Arendt, she points out that Christianity's
preoccupation with death and salvation worked against a
sense of connection to the web of life, 'and taught people
to be homeless in the world'. She quotes Arendt:

> The other-worldly attitude of the early Christian creed
> made commitment to each other's natalities less significant
> since worldly aspirations and immortal fame granted by

history were now viewed as illusory endeavours ... In
this context, human natality is no longer characterised
by its unique capacity to begin, to act, or to re-enact
but rather assumes a prominence only so far as it marks
the occasion of the announcement of a new life whose
ultimate meaning and fulfilment lay in the eternal life
to come.[6]

In this quotation Arendt is echoing something said by
St Augustine of Hippo, one of her intellectual heroes:
'*That a beginning be made, humanity was created.*' This
does not mean that there was one beginning, but that
it is in the nature of humanity always to be beginning.
Each new birth is such a beginning. The exciting thing
about our history, the thing that helps to balance all the
evil we have committed, is our passion for discovery,
for beginning again. Christ's teaching on forgiveness has
already opened for us the possibility of a new politics
that can even move us beyond great tragedy and start
again. This genius for the new beginning characterises us
in many ways, and distinguishes us from other species.
We produce new songs, new literature, new political
freedoms, even new understandings of God. In contrast
to the endless resourcefulness and creativity of humanity,
religious institutions often give the impression that they
have heard the last word on God and know God's settled
opinion on everything. But the history of humanity's
struggle with God is a history of constant surprise and
discovery. Young people are the way the world keeps
on beginning again. They are just as interested in the
meaning of life as they ever were, but they don't seem
very interested in the Church. Maybe that is because, while
God always has the potential to be new, the Church seems
to be very old. Commenting on this, Jantzen says:

even when Christianity was gradually displaced by the secularism of modernity, the rejection of connectedness with the world and the efforts to dominate the earth and its peoples were a continuation of the Christian hostility to the world in another guise. But such worldlessness, in which kinship is rejected and people see themselves as disconnected individuals, is precisely the seed-bed in which totalitarian regimes can take root.[7]

One of the conclusions Jantzen derives from this new way of looking at ourselves, and our place on the earth, is that it would help us to recover kinship with the world. She points out that this is why feminist theologians take ecology seriously, in contrast to traditional philosophy and theology, whose disembodied rationality assumes that our true home is in another world, where God resides, so that the nearer we get to God the further away we must go from the natural and animal. She contrasts this attitude with the words of the feminist, Clarice Lispector: 'I felt that animals were still one of the things close to God, a matter that has not yet invented itself, which is still warm from birth, and at the same time something that immediately stands on its feet, is thoroughly alive, that lives fully every instant, never a little at a time, that never spares itself, that never wears itself out completely.'[8]

This approach or understanding of life seems to be in marked contrast to one side of Christian thinking, which looks upon the world with gloom and suspicion, rather than with wonder and excitement. There is a counter-tradition within Christian history that we might call 'the theology of life', which I have been trying to unfold in this book. The theology of death is based on a concept of redemption or rescue. In our discussion of original sin we noticed that simply by being born we found ourselves in exile from our true homeland and needed to be rescued or redeemed. We are not where we truly belong, but are held in a captivity from which we must escape. The work of the Church is to rescue us. Since this approach touches deeply on one of our ancient human experiences, it is no surprise to find that in the mysterious collection of themes or archetypes we call the Bible, there are texts that can be read in support of this interpretation of human history. I have already discussed the archetypal power of this ancient narrative, and suggested that it is better to use lost Eden as a metaphor that expresses the human experience of discontent and failure than as a factual description of an aboriginal catastrophe. Using this approach, then heaven becomes an image of longing, just as hell becomes an image of dread, as well as a description of much that we have made of ourselves. There is another tradition within Christian theology that uses these great archetypes not as living metaphors, but as historical facts, with the consequence that they can become delusive and abusive in the use to which they are put. Eden used as a metaphor can be illuminating; Eden used as a map reference can be dangerously confusing. The theology of death takes the metaphor literally, and ends up condemning humanity to a kind of bondage that requires some sort of literal redemption. So Christ's death becomes a blood bargain with the God who demands satisfaction for humanity's original and actual sin. Christ pays the ransom price by his death, and saves those who associate themselves with his sacrifice, by claiming his self-offering as the price already paid for their redemption. The redemption theme was one of the metaphors used by Paul, and it got its meaning and power from the practice of manumission or freeing of slaves. By taking the idea of redemption literally, against the background of an equally literalist reading of the narratives of Fall and banishment from Eden, the Church began to operate the way that army special forces deal with those hostage situations that have become such a cliché of our era. Its job is to free as many hostages as it can from the clutches of the evil one and get them on board the ship of safety. So the Church becomes a life boat, launched to fish as many people as it can from the sea of destruction.

When this theological system becomes dominant, the prevailing human emotion becomes anxiety. If we accept this primitive account of the human predicament, then our anxiety is bound to be acute. I have already spent some time thinking about the ethical logic of a system that used the threat of punishment in hell after death as a way of controlling our actions during this life. We become anxious not only to avoid actions that may lead to eternal damnation; we become anxious about believing the wrong things or holding the wrong views; and *sound doctrine* becomes a life or death affair. This is the logic that lay behind the excesses of the inquisition, and all those purges that characterise the history of religion. It is expedient that a few heretics are burned or a few gay and lesbian people are condemned to loveless self-hatred, rather than that God's special people perish through the infections of false teaching. Theologies of anxiety see God as judge and executioner and the Church as the criminal investigation division. It becomes more important to root out evil than to promote good. Contrary to the words of Jesus in the parable of the tares and wheat, when he told us to let both grow together till the harvest, much energy is spent pulling out weeds from the Church's fields. Neurotic believers become convinced that if they follow the advice of Jesus and leave them alone, the weeds will take over the whole outfit. Religious anxiety of this sort always hates the devil more than it loves God. It creates churches that are exclusive in their self-understanding, and proclaim that there is no salvation outside their walls. Yet, it was this great engine of anxiety that promoted the remarkable successes of Christian mission. The urge to save as many as possible from the wrath of God was a powerful spur to missionary heroism; and the fear of that same wrath has always been a powerful incentive to conversion.

Theologies of anxiety have considerable strengths. The main one is the coherence of the system they proclaim. Once we accept the premises on which the message is based, the logic is powerful and persuasive. It can be learnt easily and taught effectively. It is, essentially, a product, a package that can be explained to the sales force. Its second strength is that it can be remarkably successful in inculcating particular systems of behaviour. The Protestant work ethic is an example of how a particular version of the theology of anxiety led to a powerful ethic of duty, so that the compulsion remains long after the theological premise on which it was based has been abandoned. The other strength that is worth noting is the sacrificial lives of those who have committed themselves to this particular theological approach. It has taken them to the ends of the earth and prompted them to extraordinary feats of human endurance. Those of us who cannot admire the motivation that lies behind such heroism often find ourselves admiring those who gave their lives in its service.

Fortunately, this is not the only theological approach that has been developed in Christian history. There has always been a theology of life that emphasised the good-ness of creation, rather than its fallen state, and the fact that God chose to dwell in its midst and taste its bitter-sweet joys. These rival theologies inevitably remind us of the old challenge that asks whether the glass is half empty or half full. It is a question of whether we emphasise the sheer gifted joy of being alive or the undoubted fact that we are always capable of destroying our own peace and polluting our own habitation. The original blessing approach coheres well with a theology of natality and flourishing. Grace and the celebration of life, rather than dread and the fear of death, become the motivators of life and action. The message does not warn people how to be saved out of this wicked world; it invites them to feel at home in it, to reverence it, and to practise the disciplines of sharing its good things with others, particularly with the poor of the earth. That is why it is far from true that the theology of life lacks challenge and rigour. It calls us to courageous action against all that spoils the joy of life and the sacredness of creation. It calls us to a politics of justice because one of the scandals of history is the way the powerful have colonised creation for themselves and yoked its children into slavery. The theology of life calls us, in the language of the prayer of Jesus, to build the kingdom of God on earth as it is in heaven.

Compared with the dramatic theologies of anxiety and fear, the theology of life suffers from presentational difficulties. The theology of death is schematically logical, once you accept the horrifying premise on which it is based. That is why it is easy to plant it as a complete system in the hearts and minds of its practitioners. Its negative use is also easy to apply, which is why its practitioners are able to operate theological tests that screen out those who do not adhere to the purity of the system. Theological creativity is not required and is, in fact, mistrusted in the officers of the system, because it is already perfectly articulated. The only creativity that is permitted is at the rhetorical level, where the speaker's art may be used to commend the system. And the Grand Inquisitor was right, human beings do find these complete systems to be a powerful antidote to anxiety, so it is no surprise that the history of religion and politics is full of them, all competing with each other to have the last word. T.S. Eliot constantly reminded us that humankind cannot bear too much reality, so the historic prevalence of these absolute systems should not surprise or dismay us. Perhaps those of us who can no longer adhere to any of them should stop wasting our emotional and intellectual energy in combating them and, instead, should turn our attention to the positive promotion of the kind of vision of life I have been propounding in this book. What, then, should be the defining characteristics of a positive theology of life? I would like to suggest several elements.

There is a famous passage in Bede's *Ecclesiastical History* in which he gives an account of the conversion of King Edwin of Northumbria. After bishop Paulinus pleads the case for Christianity, an old noble speaks:

The present life of men on earth, O king, as compared with the whole length of time, which is unknowable to us, seems to me to be like this: as if, when you are sitting at dinner with your chiefs and ministers in wintertime ... one of the sparrows from outside flew very quickly through the hall; as if it came in one door and soon went out through another. In that actual time it is indoors it is not touched by winter's storm; but yet the tiny period of calm is over in a moment, and having come out of the winter it soon returns to the winter and slips out of your sight. Man's life appears to be more or less like this; and of what may follow it, or what preceded it, we are absolutely ignorant.[9]

Our lives are longer than a sparrow's, but they are brief enough and all too soon we go back out into the night. Given the brevity and beauty of our passage through life, it is a pity not to pay attention to the earth and its creatures. The traditional name for this process is prayer or contemplation. One of the great gifts of organised religion to the world has been the provision of men and women who have had this gift of attention or contemplation. One of the most realised versions of the priest who sees into the depths of things was Gilles in Helen Waddell's novel about Peter Abelard from which I have already quoted. Here is another quotation:

He laid down Abelard's close-written sheet on his knee, and his eye travelled to the window. The sun was still low in the east: why, wondered Gilles, should this level light transfigure the earth, beyond any magic of sunrise or sunset? He saw the bare trees of the Terrain beyond the eastern wall of the cloister, the swift grey current of the Seine, and across the narrow strait the Ile Notre Dame with its black piles of wood and turf, the grass beyond them a strange passionate green. There is more colour, he thought, in November than there is in August, except in water. The river knows it may be frozen in a week, and it runs ice-grey already. For water dies: the earth never. Perhaps, thought Gilles, it was because he himself was in his November, and the last day of it too, he added with a crooked smile, that the autumn seemed to him richer than any spring, and this pale persistent sunlight had a kind of heroic tenderness. There is no memory in spring he thought, not even the memory of other springs: but a November day of faint sunlight and emerald moss remembers all things, the wild promise of the January days, snow-broth in February, violets in March, new-mown hay in June, dew-wet mint trodden underfoot in August nights, the harvest moon in September, the hunter's moon in October. Prudentius, he thought, was the November of the poets: Prudentius remembering

> How many times the rose
> Returned after the snows.[10]

The swiftness of our days and the acknowledgement that we are always old enough to die, should prompt us to live passionately and intentionally and not waste the one life we have. There is a haunting sequence in Sergio Leone's great homage to the Hollywood gangster movie, *Once Upon a Time in America*, that captures the sadness of a wasted life. The film is the story of a group of Jewish boys who meet in the twenties in Manhattan's Lower East Side. The story concentrates on Max, played by James Wood, and Noodles, played by Robert De Niro, both of whom have loved Deborah, played by Elizabeth McGovern, since they were children. The gang is destroyed in 1933, but Noodles escapes and goes into hiding for 35 years. He returns to New York in 1968 after receiving a mystifying letter. Asked what he'd been doing during all those years in hiding Noodles replies, 'I went to bed early, nights.' De Niro packs the simple line with the sense of a lifetime of loss.

If life is a stage on which we act our brief part, then death is the prompter in the wings. In a lecture on painting reported in the *Guardian* in August 2000, Peter Berger suggested that art was a battle with our own transience: 'The portraitist contests the mortality of his sitter. The landscape painter contests the ceaseless movement of nature; the history painter the forgetting of history; and the still life painter the dispersal of objects. His antagonists are decay, the bailiff and the junk merchant.' All art is trying to get us to pay attention, to look at life and love it before we go from the fire-lit banqueting hall out into the winter's darkness.

Don Cupitt has described contemplation as 'attention to the forthcoming of Be-ing'. He suggests that one way to do this is by watching the movement of a cloud for ten minutes.[11] Another way into this kind of rapturous attention is through the poets, who are the geniuses of contemplation. Poetry is the gift of priestly attention. Here are two examples. The first comes from C. Day Lewis, an unfashionable poet at the moment, whom the academic critics define as not being quite first rate. He speaks to me, however, and I have found wisdom as well as pity in his poems. The one I am about to quote may be slight and unimportant, but it is a good example of a kind of attention to the world I think of as prayer or intrinsic gratitude.

> In a sun-crazed orchard
> Busy with blossomings
> This loafer, unaware of
> What toil or weather brings,
> Lumpish sleeps – a chrysalis
> Waiting, no doubt, for wings.

> And when he does get active,
> It's not for business – no
> Bee-lines to thyme or heather,
> No earnest to-and-fro
> Of thrushes: pure caprice tells him
> Where and how to go.

> All he can ever do
> Is to be entrancing,
> So that a child may think,
> Upon a chalk-blue chancing,
> 'Today was special. I met
> A piece of the sky dancing.'[12]

The second is from Norman MacCaig:

> Beside one loch, a hind's neat skeleton,
> Beside another, a boat pulled high and dry:
> Two neat geometries drawn in the weather:
> Two things already dead and still to die.
>
> I passed them every summer, rod in hand,
> Skirting the bright blue or the spitting gray,
> And, every summer, saw how the bleached timbers
> Gaped wider and the neat ribs fell away.
>
> Time adds one malice to another one –
> Now you'd look very close before you knew
> If it's the boat that ran, the hind went sailing.
> So many summers, and I have lived them too.[13]

To avoid sentimentality it is important that this prayer of attention should not just be focused on nature; we should look at one another with the same expectation of revelation, especially when we look into alien or frightening worlds. One way of doing this is to buy *The Big Issue* from every vendor we meet. Apart from being a personal act of redistributive justice, the real point is to look into the eyes of the homeless and say something that connects us to them. Even if we have no money, we can give them our attention as we apologise. Many of them will find that as important a gift as the coin we can absently slip into their hands. And we should pay attention to people enjoying themselves, especially to lovers and friends sharing affection or amusement in public. Cities are the best places for this because we can encounter many worlds as we walk through them. I am quoting too many things, but I cannot resist that famous incident when Thomas Merton describes a walk along the street in Louisville, Kentucky:

> At the corner of Fourth and Walnut, in the centre of the shopping district, I was suddenly overwhelmed with the realisation that I loved all these people, that they were mine and I theirs, that we could not be alien to one another even though we were total strangers. It was like waking from a dream of separateness, of spurious self-isolation in a special world, the world of renunciation and supposed holiness. The sense of liberation from an illusory difference was such a relief and joy to me that I almost laughed out loud.[14]

If attention is the first duty of those who want to love the world, then repentance must be the second. The truth that lies at the heart of the theology of death is the damage we do to one another. In this book I have used the Holocaust as the great paradigm of human evil, but there are many others that would have done just as well, such as the long history of the slave trade. One of the paradise longings of humanity is the desire to rewind what Hannah Arendt called the irreversible processes of history, to make it as though it had never happened, to bring back that deed, to recall that word, to get back to the time before the serpent put it into our mind to destroy Eden. One of the best examples of this sorrow comes not from an agent of such grief, but from one of its victims. It is a poem from the Holocaust by Dan Pagis:

All right, gentlemen who cry blue murder as always,
nagging miracle makers,
quiet!
Everything will be returned to its place,
paragraph after paragraph.
The scream back into the throat.
The gold teeth back into the gums.
The terror.
The smoke back to the tin chimney and further on
    and inside
back to the hollow of the bones,
and already you will be covered with skin and sinews and
    you will live,
look, you will have your lives back,
sit in the living room, read the evening paper.
Here you are. Nothing is too late.
As to the yellow star: immediately
it will be torn from your chest
and will emigrate
to the sky.[15]

That poem echoes Ezekiel's vision of the valley of desola-
tion, filled with the dead bones of the people of Israel. It
is an apt *eikon* of the horrors of our history. It summons
up not only the slave trade and the Holocaust, but the
Killing Fields of Pol Pot's Cambodia, and the Rwandan and
Bosnian genocides of our own day. One of the tasks of an
honest theology of life will be to remember those crimes
and cry for collective repentance. As humans, we are
implicated in them all, but our particular tribal pathologies
will necessitate specific acts of sorrow and repentance.

But repentance cannot be the final word. The final
word must be about the remaking of the earth. This is
the task to which those who want to listen have been
summoned by Jesus. John Dominic Crossan makes an

important distinction in his interpretation of the work of Jesus. He suggests that Jesus might have turned from the apocalyptic idea of supernatural intervention and to a new eschatology of human struggle. Let me draw this book to a close by quoting what he says on the subject:

> The apocalyptic is a future Kingdom dependent on the overpowering action of God moving to restore justice and peace to an earth ravished by injustice and oppression. Believers can, at the very most, prepare or persuade, implore or assist its arrival, but its accomplishment is consigned to divine power alone. And despite a serene vagueness about specifics and details, its consummation would be objectively visible and tangible to all, believers and unbelievers alike, but with appropriately different fates. The sapiential Kingdom[16] looks to the present rather than the future and imagines how one could live here and now within an already or always available divine dominion. One enters that Kingdom by wisdom or goodness, by virtue, justice, or freedom. It is a style of life for now rather than a hope of life for the future. This is therefore an ethical Kingdom, but it must be absolutely insisted that it could be just as eschatological as was the apocalyptic Kingdom. Its ethics could, for instance, challenge contemporary morality to its depths.[17]

Such a kingdom is just as world-denying as the theology of death, but the world it denies is not this world as such, the only world we know, but the usurpation of it by the forces of evil and injustice that claim it as their own. To commit ourselves, often against all worldly logic, to the task of bringing in that new world of righteousness is the best of what is left of the vision for which Jesus died. I have already quoted from Albert Schweitzer's book in which he searched for the real man of Nazareth.

Schweitzer came to the conclusion that Jesus had tried to force God to intervene to heal our wounded world by deliberately accepting martyrdom in Jerusalem. He had died mistaken and forsaken. This tragic conclusion drove Schweitzer from the study of theology into the work of practical love. He wrote of this period in his life:

> What seemed to my friends the most irrational thing in my plan was that I wanted to go to Africa, not as a missionary, but as a doctor, and thus when already thirty years of age burdened myself with a long period of laborious study. I wanted to be a doctor that I might be able to work without having to talk. For years I had been giving myself out in words, and it was with joy that I had followed the calling of theological teacher and preacher. But this new form of activity I could not represent to myself as being talking about the religion of love, but only as an actual putting it into practice.[18]

In 1913 he went with his wife to Lambaréné in what was then the French colony of Gabon as a doctor. He spent his life there, no longer talking about Jesus but still trying to follow him. The last words of his mighty book are the ones with which I want to conclude this little one.

> He comes to us as One unknown, without a name, as of old, by the lake-side, He came to those men who knew Him not. He speaks to us the same word: 'Follow thou me!' and sets us to the tasks which He has to fulfil for our time. He commands. And to those who obey Him, whether they be wise or simple, He will reveal Himself in the toils, the conflicts, the sufferings which they shall pass through in His fellowship, and, as an ineffable mystery, they shall learn in their own experience Who He Is.[19]

This is what you should do: Love the earth and sun and animals,
        despise riches, give alms to everyone who asks,
            stand up for the stupid and crazy,
        devote your income and labour to others, hate tyrants,
            argue not concerning God,
        have patience and indulgence toward the people,
        re-examine all you have been told in school or church
                or any book,
            dismiss what insults your very soul,
        and your flesh shall become a great poem.

Walt Whitman
From the preface to the 1855
edition of *Leaves of Grass*

Afterword

A friend once accused me of leaving no thought unpublished. It was a valid criticism. I have written too many books in my time, some of which now embarrass me, though they serve to remind me of the many times I have changed my mind over the years about important matters, especially religion, and that is a salutary lesson to learn. Another limitation worth mentioning is that I am incapable of writing objective, heavily researched books about religion. This is because I do not have a scholarly mind and I am easily bored. But for me religion was never just a subject to get up with study. It was always a battle for meaning, including the meaning of my own life. Karl Marx was once asked by an American journalist to answer the question: '"What is?" . . . to which . . . he replied: "Struggle!" At first it seemed as though I had heard the echo of despair but peradventure it was the law of life.' That has certainly been my experience of religion; and sometimes it has felt like a fight for my spiritual life.

Sometimes the struggle has been with interpretations of religion I have found cruel and offensive. Sometimes the struggle has been with my own understanding of God. And sometimes it has been a struggle to distil and commend to others what is of enduring value in Christianity, which is what I was trying to do when I wrote this book. It is the nearest I ever came to writing a systematic study of religion, but it is probably better described as 'engaged' rather than scholarly.

And how could I not be engaged with what I was writing?

The most important influence on my life has been Jesus of Nazareth, a first-century Jew of definite but elusive genius who was later divinised by his followers in the early Church. The question that has nagged at me for decades is the one that also nagged at Plato: is an ethic good because it is commended by God? Or is it commended by God because it is good? The Jesus version of that conundrum is just as taxing. Are we challenged to follow Jesus because we think he is God? Or do we think he is God because we are challenged to follow him? The answer to both the Platonic and Jesus versions of the question boils down either to the primacy of action over theory or theory over action. Is it more important to do the right thing than to believe the right thing? Or is it always right belief that guarantees right action? How are we to decide?

The Latin root of the verb in question gives us a clue: *decidere* means to cut. What we are invited to do is to cut the knot we've tangled ourselves in and act; to stop messing around and *do* something. The useful demotic phrase 'cut the crap' comes to mind here, something Jesus certainly did at the end of Matthew's gospel in the parable of the sheep and the goats. The sheep that acted but did not theorise proved by their actions that they'd got the theory right; while the goats that theorised but did not act proved by their lack of action that they'd got the theory wrong. In *Doubts and Loves* I was trying to follow the logic of that parable by separating Christian theory from Christian action. There is no doubt that Jesus fervently believed in God, and believed that his God was the prompter of his challenge to the powerful who oppressed the poor and weak. He stood firmly in the line of the other Hebrew prophets who had told the astounded Israelites that God was not interested in their worship – and actually hated it – but wanted, instead, justice for the oppressed. It's the same tight knot that calls for the same sharp knife; or as Jesus put it earlier in Matthew:

Not everyone that saith unto me, Lord, Lord, shall enter into the kingdom of heaven; but he that doeth the will of my Father which is in heaven. 7.21

The beauty of that approach is that it takes a lot of unnecessary struggle out of the God question. God loves justice, we are told, because he himself is just, so to act justly is to do his will *whether we know it or not* – and God doesn't seem to mind either way. For the good person, justice and mercy are their own justification. Good people need no external prod in their side to goad them into doing what is right. The paradox is this: if God exists, whether we believe it or not, by acting justly we are doing his will anyway.

You can almost hear the God of Jesus chuckle at the simplicity of it all. If that is all that is left of Christianity, it is more than enough.

RICHARD HOLLOWAY
EDINBURGH, 2019

Notes

Chapter 1

1. Richard Dawkins, *River out of Eden*, Weidenfeld and Nicolson, London, 1955, p.96.
2. Friedrich Nietzsche, *The Will to Power*, Vintage, New York, 1968, p.12.
3. Dennis Potter, *Seeing the Blossom*, Faber and Faber, London, 1994, p.5.
4. Callum G. Brown, *The Death of Christian Britain*, Routledge, London, 2000.
5. Ibid., pp.196–7.
6. Françoise-Marie Arouet de Voltaire, *Reflections on Religion*, quoted in *The Portable Enlightenment Reader*, Penguin, New York, 1995, p.131.

Chapter 2

1. Friedrich Nietzsche, *Human All Too Human*, section 5, *The Portable Nietzsche*, Penguin, New York, 1968, p.52.
2. Matthew Tindal, *Christianity as Old as the Creation* (1733), quoted in Roy Porter, *Enlightenment*, Allen Lane, the Penguin Press, London, 2000, p.113.
3. Emily Dickinson, 'This World is not Conclusion', *The Complete Poems*, Little, Brown and Company, Toronto, 1960, poem 501.
4. John Hick, *The Fifth Dimension*, One Word, Oxford, 1999, pp.42–3.
5. Ibid.
6. Don Cupitt, *Solar Ethics*, SCM, London, 1995.

Chapter 3

1. Shakespeare, *The Winter's Tale* [IV.3].
2. Marcus Borg, 'Revisioning Christianity', at a conference in St Andrews in September 1999.
3. W.B. Yeats, 'The Circus Animals' Desertion', *The Poems*, Everyman, London, 1994, p.235.
4. Brenda Maddox, *George's Ghosts*, Picador, London, 1999, pp.127, 128.
5. W.B. Yeats, 'The Circus Animals' Desertion', *The Poems*, Everyman, London, 1994, p.235.

Chapter 4

1. Thomas Khun, *The Structure of Scientific Revolutions*, University of Chicago Press, 1970.
2. Ibid., p.2.
3. Ibid., p.10.
4. Ibid., p.xii.
5. Imran Javaid, *Thomas Kuhn: Paradigms Die Hard*. hcs.harvard.edu/~hsr/hsr/winter97/kuhn.html.
6. This is why the most eloquent exponent of this type of philosophy, Richard Rorty, gave the title *Contingency, Irony, and Solidarity* (Cambridge, 1989) to one of his books.
7. Richard Rorty, *Philosophy and Social Hope*, Penguin, London, 1999, p.148.
8. Paul Tillich, *Dynamics of Faith*, Harper Torchbooks, New York, 1958, p.45.
9. Ibid., p.112.
10. Exodus, 32.2–4.
11. Paul Tillich, *Dynamics of Faith*, Harper Torchbooks, New York, 1958, p.49.
12. Ibid., p.49.
13. Ibid., pp.50–1.
14. Ibid., pp.51–2.

Chapter 5

1. André Schwarz-Bart, *The Last of the Just*, Penguin, London, 1977, pp.373ff.
2. W.B. Yeats, 'He Wishes for the Cloths of Heaven', *Collected Poems*, Everyman, London 1994, p.90.
3. A.N. Wilson, *Paul*, Sinclair-Stevenson, London, 1997, p.73.
4. *American Negro Spirituals*, vol.1, The Viking Press, New York, 1951, p.51.
5. Friedrich Nietzsche, *Daybreak*, section 109, *The Nietzsche Reader*, Penguin, London, 1977, p.156.

Chapter 6

1. Voltaire, *Philosophical Dictionary*, Penguin, London, 1972, p.61.
2. Gospel of Luke, 16:24, 25.
3. Voltaire, *Philosophical Dictionary*, p.60.
4. Peter Brown, *Augustine of Hippo*, Faber and Faber, London, 1967, pp.388, 389.
5. Sigmund Freud, *Civilisation, Society and Religion*, Penguin, London, 1991, p.289.
6. Plato, *Symposium*, Oxford World Classics, 1994, p.25.
7. Ibid., p.28.
8. A.E. Housman, *Poetry and Prose: A Selection*, Hutchinson, London, 1972, p.86.

Chapter 7

1. James Joyce, *Portrait of the Artist as a Young Man*, Penguin, London, pp.121–2.
2. Friedrich Nietzsche, *On the Genealogy of Morals*, Oxford University Press, 1996, I.15.
3. Psalm 88.3–5.
4. Isaiah, 14.1–20.
5. Gita, VI.45, quoted in John Hick, *The Fifth Dimension*, p.57.
6. Hick, *The Fifth Dimension*.
7. Ibid., p.58.

8. Paul Tillich, *The Protestant Era*, Nisbet, 1955, p.xxxv.ff.
9. André Schwarz-Bart, *The Last of the Just*, pp.382–3.
10. George Steiner, *Errata*, Phoenix, London, 1997, pp.57–60.
11. Ibid.
12. Ibid.
13. Ibid.

Chapter 8

1. W.H. Auden, *About the House*, Faber, London, 1958, p.27.
2. Paul, Letter to the Romans, chapter 7.15–24.
3. Paul, Letter to the Galations, chapter 1.13–14.
4. Gospel of Luke, 6.1–11.
5. Gospel of Mark, 2.23–27.
6. Romans, 8.1–4.
7. *The Essential Tillich*, University of Chicago Press, 1987, p.200.
8. Ibid. p.201.
9. Ibid.
10. Friedrich Nietzsche, *The Genealogy of Morals*, 3rd essay, section 15, *The Basic Writings of Nietzsche*, The Modern Library, New York, 1992, p.563.

Chapter 9

1. Letter of James, 2.19.
2. David Hume, *The Natural History of Religion*, edited by H.E. Root, Stanford, 1957, section III.
3. Cited in John Dominic Crossan, *The Birth of Christianity*, Harper, San Francisco, 1999, p.488.
4. John Bowker, *Is God a Virus?* SPCK, London, 1995, p.176.
5. *The Autobiography of Martin Luther King Jr*, Clayborne Carson (ed.), Time Warner Books, New York, 1998, p.52.

Chapter 10

1. Raymond Brown, *An Adult Christ at Christmas*, The Liturgical Press, Collegeville Minnesota, 1978, p.9.
2. Gospel of Matthew, 2:1–21.
3. Letter to the Hebrews, 9.1–15.

4. Raymond Brown, *An Introduction to the New Testament*, Doubleday, New York, 1997, p.283.
5. Revelation, 20:1–3.

Chapter 11

1. John Donne, 'Satyre III', *Complete Poetry and Selected Prose*, The Nonesuch Press, London, 1941, p.129.
2. W.B. Yeats, 'The Second Coming', *The Poems*, Everyman, London, 1994, p.235.
3. George Mackay Brown, *An Orkney Tapestry*, Victor Gollancz, London, 1969, p.11.
4. John Dominic Crossan, *The Historical Jesus*, Harper, San Francisco, 1992, p.105.
5. Raymond Brown, *The Emergence of the Christian Church*, Welcome Recordings, 6 Upper Aston Hall Lane, Hawarden, Flintshire, Wales, 1998.
6. Gospel of John, 11.47–50 (The King James Version).
7. Gospel of Matthew, 18.22.
8. Hannah Arendt, *The Portable Hannah Arendt*, Penguin, New York, 2000, p.17.
9. Ibid.
10. John Dominic Crossan, *The Essential Jesus*, HarperCollins, San Francisco, 1995, pp.26, 30, 51, 123.
11. Gospel of John, 1.10–11.
12. Alasdair MacIntyre, *After Virtue*, University of Notre Dame Press, 1981, p.103.
13. Dominic Crossan, *The Historical Jesus*, p.424.
14. Quoted in Richard Rorty, *Philosophy and Social Hope*, Penguin, London, 1999, pp.xxii–xxiii.

Chapter 12

1. Friedrich Nietzsche, *Human, All-too-Human*, section 224, in *The Portable Nietzsche*, Penguin, New York, 1976, p.54.
2. Ibid.
3. Richard Rorty, *Philosophy and Social Hope*, Penguin, London, 1999, p.117.

4. Gospel of Mark, 15.26.
5. Albert Schweitzer, *The Quest of the Historical Jesus*, SCM, London, 1981, pp.368, 369.
6. Jorge Luis Borges, 'Luke XXIII', translated from the Spanish by Mark Strand in *Selected Poems*, Penguin Putnam, New York, 2000.

Chapter 13

1. Nietzsche's aside.
2. Friedrich Nietzsche, *Beyond Good and Evil*, section 258, *Basic Writings of Nietzsche*, The Modern Library, New York, 1992, p.392.
3. George Steiner, *Errata*, Phoenix, London, 1997, pp.13–14.
4. Ibid.
5. Nietzsche's aside.
6. Friedrich Nietzsche, *On the Genealogy of Morals*, First essay, section 10, *Basic Writings of Nietzsche*, The Modern Library, New York, 1992, p.475.
7. Ibid., Second essay, section 16, pp.520–1.
8. Francis Wheen, *Karl Marx*, Fourth Estate, London, 1999, p.383.
9. John Dominic Crossan, *Jesus*, HarperCollins, San Francisco, 1995, p.105.
10. Wheen, *Karl Marx*, p.14.
11. Karl Marx, *The German Ideology*, from *The Portable Karl Marx*, Penguin, London, 1983, p.162.
12. Cecil Frances Alexander, 'All Things Bright and Beautiful', in *Hymns Ancient and Modern*, Canterbury Press, Norwich, 1988, number 116.
13. J.K. Galbraith, *The Good Society*, Sinclair-Stevenson, 1996, pp.61–2.
14. Wheen, *Karl Marx*, p.300.
15. Ibid.
16. Richard Rorty, *Philosophy and Social Hope*, Penguin, London, 1999, p.248.

Chapter 14

1. Gospel of Luke, 15.11–32.

2. Helen Waddell, *Peter Abelard*, Constable, London, 1939, p.125.
3. Hannah Arendt, from *Labour, Work, Action*, in *The Portable Hannah Arendt*, Penguin, London, 2000, pp.180–1.

Chapter 15

1. Max Weber, *Essays in Economic Sociology*, Princeton University Press, 1999, p.106.
2. Abraham Lincoln, *Letter to Horace Greeley*, 22 August 1862, quoted in *Encyclopaedia Britannica*, London, 1962, Vol.14, p.143.
3. Fyodor Dostoevsky, *The Brothers Karamazov*, Penguin, London, 1969, vol.1, pp.288ff.
4. Ibid., p.308.
5. Grace M. Jantzen, *Becoming Divine*, Manchester University Press, 1998.
6. As quoted in Jantzen, *Becoming Divine*, p.151.
7. Ibid.
8. Ibid., p.152.
9. The Venerable Bede, *Ecclesiastical History*, 2.13.
10. Helen Waddell, *Peter Abelard*, Constable, London, 1939, p.202.
11. Don Cupitt, *Philosophy's Own Religion*, SCM, London, 2000, p.140.
12. C. Day Lewis, 'This Loafer', in *The Complete Poems*, Sinclair-Stevenson, London, 1992, p.636.
13. Norman MacCaig, 'So Many Summers', in *Collected Poems*, Chatto and Windus, London, 1993, p.220.
14. Thomas Merton, *Conjectures of a Guilty Bystander*, Doubleday, New York, 1989, p.156.
15. Dan Pagis, 'Draft of a Reparation Agreement', in *Modern Poems on the Bible* (ed. David Curzon), The Jewish Publication Society, Philadelphia, 1994, p.249.
16. Crossan's term for a programme of social and political transformation on earth.
17. John Dominic Crossan, *The Historical Jesus*, p.292.
18. Albert Schweitzer, *Out of My Life and Thought: An Autobiography*, Holt, New York, 1933, pp.114–15.
19. Albert Schweitzer, *The Quest of the Historical Jesus*, SCM, London, 1981, p.401.

Select Bibliography

Amichai, Yehuda, *Selected Poetry*, University of California Press, Berkeley, 1996

Arendt, Hannah, *The Portable Hannah Arendt*, Penguin, New York, 2000

Brown, Callum G., *The Death of Christian Britain*, Routledge, London, 2000

Brown, Peter, *Augustine of Hippo*, Faber and Faber, London, 1967

Brown, Raymond, *An Introduction to the New Testament*, Doubleday, New York, 1997

Crossan, John Dominic, *The Historical Jesus*, HarperCollins, San Francisco, 1992

Crossan, John Dominic, *The Essential Jesus*, HarperCollins, San Francisco, 1995

Crossan, John Dominic, *Jesus*, HarperCollins, San Francisco, 1995

Crossan, John Dominic, *The Birth of Christianity*, HarperCollins, San Francisco, 1999

Cupitt, Don, *Solar Ethics*, SCM, London, 1995

Cuppit, Don, *Philosophy's Own Religion*, SCM, London, 2000

Dawkins, Richard, *River out of Eden*, Weidenfeld and Nicolson, 1955

Freud, Sigmund, *Civilisation, Society and Religion*, Penguin, London, 1991

Galbraith, J. K., *The Good Society*, Sinclair-Stevenson, London, 1996

Hick, John, *The Fifth Dimension*, One Word, Oxford, 1999

Hume, David, *The Natural History of Religion*, ed. H.E. Root, Stanford, 1957

Jantzen, Grace M., *Becoming Divine*, Manchester University Press, 1998

Khun, Thomas, *The Structure of Scientific Revolutions*, University of Chicago Press, 1970

Maddox, Brenda, *George's Ghosts*, Picador, London, 1999

Marx, Karl, *The Portable Karl Marx*, Penguin, London, 1983

Nietzsche, Friedrich, *The Will to Power*, Vintage, New York, 1968

Nietzsche, Friedrich, *The Portable Nietzsche*, Penguin, New York, 1976

Nietzsche, Friedrich, *The Nietzsche Reader*, Penguin, London, 1977

Nietzsche, Friedrich, *Basic Writings of Nietzsche*, The Modern Library, New York, 1992

Nietzsche, Friedrich, *On the Genealogy of Morals*, Oxford University Press, 1996

Plato, *Symposium*, Oxford World Classics, 1994

Porter, Roy, *The Enlightenment*, Allen Lane, the Penguin Press, London, 2000

Rorty, Richard, *The Contingency, Irony and Solidarity*, Cambridge University Press, 1987

Rorty, Richard, *Philosophy and Social Hope*, Penguin, London, 1999

Schwarz-Bart, André, *The Last of the Just*, Penguin, London, 1977

Schweitzer, Albert, *Out of My Life and Thought: An Autobiography*, Holt, New York, 1933

Schweitzer, Albert, *The Quest of the Historical Jesus*, SCM, London, 1981

Steiner, George, *Errata*, Phoenix, London, 1997

Tillich, Hannah, *From Time to Time*, Stein and Day, 1974

Tillich, Paul, *The Protestant Era*, Nisbet, 1955

Tillich, Paul, *Dynamics of Faith*, Harper Torchbooks, New York, 1958

Tillich, Paul, *The Essential Tillich*, University of Chicago Press, 1987

Voltaire, François-Marie Arouet, *Philosophical Dictionary*, Penguin, London, 1972

Voltaire, François-Marie Arouet, *The Portable Enlightenment Reader*, Penguin, New York, 1995

Voltaire, François-Marie Arouet, *The Portable Voltaire*, Penguin, New York, 1997

Waddell, Helen, *Peter Abelard*, Constable, London, 1939

Wheen, Francis, *Karl Marx*, Fourth Estate, London 1999

Wilson, A. N., *Paul*, Sinclair-Stevenson, London, 1997

Index

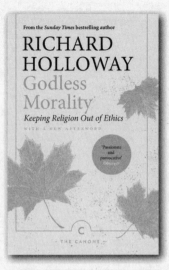

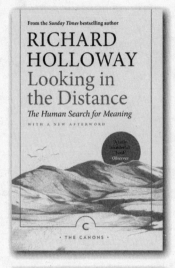

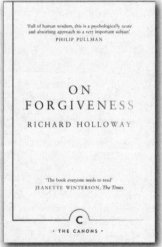

'A very wise man indeed. Inspiring [and] fascinating' FAY WELDON

CANON❚GATE